POST-SYNODAL
APOSTOLIC EXHORTATION
ECCLESIA IN AFRICA
OF THE HOLY FATHER
JOHN PAUL II
TO THE BISHOPS
PRIESTS AND DEACONS
MEN AND WOMEN RELIGIOUS
AND ALL THE LAY FAITHFUL
ON THE CHURCH IN AFRICA
AND ITS EVANGELIZING MISSION
TOWARDS THE YEAR 2000

Publication No. 5-059
United States Catholic Conference
Washington, D.C.
ISBN 1-57455-059-4

Text and format from
LIBRERIA EDITRICE VATICANA
Vatican City

CONTENTS

INTRODUCTION

CHAPTER I
AN HISTORIC MOMENT OF GRACE

CHAPTER II
THE CHURCH IN AFRICA

CHAPTER III

EVANGELIZATION AND INCULTURATION

CHAPTER VI

BUILDING THE KINGDOM OF GOD

CHAPTER VII

"YOU SHALL BE MY WITNESSES
TO THE ENDS OF THE EARTH"

CONCLUSION

INTRODUCTION

1. THE CHURCH WHICH IS IN AFRICA celebrated with joy and hope its faith in the Risen Christ during the four weeks of the Special Assembly for Africa of the Synod of Bishops. Memories of this event are still fresh in the minds of the whole Ecclesial Community.

Faithful to the tradition of the first centuries of Christianity in Africa, the Pastors of this Continent, in communion with the Successor of the Apostle Peter and members of the Episcopal College from other parts of the world, held a Synod which was intended to be an occasion of hope and resurrection, at the very moment when human events seemed to be tempting Africa to discouragement and despair.

The Synod Fathers, assisted by qualifed representatives of the clergy, religious and laity, subjected to a detailed and realistic study the lights and shadows, the challenges and future prospects of evangelization in Africa on the threshold of the Third Millennium of the Christian faith.

The members of the Synodal Assembly asked me to bring to the attention of the whole Church the results of their reflections and prayers, discussions and exchanges.[1] With joy and gratitude to

---

[1] Cf. *Propositio* 1.

the Lord I accepted this request and today, at the very moment when, in communion with the Pastors and faithful of the Catholic Church in Africa, I begin the celebration phase of the Special Assembly for Africa, I am promulgating the text of this Post-Synodal Apostolic Exhortation, the result of an intense and prolonged collegial endeavour.

But before describing what developed in the course of the Synod, I consider it helpful to go back, if only briefly, over the various stages of an event of such decisive importance for the Church in Africa.

The Council

2.   The Second Vatican Ecumenical Council can certainly be considered, from the point of view of the history of salvation, as the cornerstone of the present century which is now rapidly approaching the Third Millennium. In the context of that great event, the Church of God in Africa experienced true moments of grace. Indeed, the idea of some form of meeting of the African Bishops to discuss the evangelization of the Continent dates back to the time of the Council. That historic event was truly the crucible of collegiality and a specific expression of the *affective* and *effective* communion of the worldwide Episcopate. At the Council, the Bishops sought to identify appropriate means of better sharing and making more effective their care for all the Churches (cf. *2 Cor* 11:28), and for this purpose they began to plan

suitable structures at the national, regional and continental level.

The Symposium of Episcopal Conferences of Africa and Madagascar

3. It is in such a climate that the Bishops of Africa and Madagascar present at the Council decided to establish their own General Secretariat with the task of coordinating their interventions, in order to present to the Council Fathers, as far as possible, a common point of view. This initial cooperation among the Bishops of Africa later became permanent in the creation in Kampala of the *Symposium of Episcopal Conferences of Africa and Madagascar* (SECAM). This took place in July-August 1969, during the visit of Pope Paul VI to Uganda — the first of a Pope to Africa in modern times.

The convocation of the Special Assembly for Africa of the Synod of Bishops

4. The General Assemblies of the Synod of Bishops, held regularly from 1967 onwards, offered valuable opportunities for the Church in Africa to make its voice heard in the Church throughout the world. Thus, at the Second Ordinary General Assembly (1971), the Synod Fathers from Africa happily took the occasion offered them to appeal for greater justice in the world. The Third Ordinary General Assembly (1974), on evangelization in the modern world, made pos-

sible a special study of the problems of evangelization in Africa. It was then that the Bishops of the Continent present at the Synod issued an important message entitled *Promoting Evangelization in Co-Responsibility*.[2] Shortly afterwards, during the Holy Year of 1975, SECAM convoked its own plenary meeting in Rome, in order to examine the subject of evangelization.

5. Subsequently, from 1977 to 1983, some Bishops, priests, consecrated persons, theologians and lay people expressed a desire for an *African Council* or *African Synod,* which would have the task of evaluating evangelization in Africa vis-à-vis the great choices to be made regarding the Continent's future. I gladly welcomed and encouraged the idea of the "working together, in one form or another", of the whole African Episcopate in order "to study the religious problems that concern the whole Continent".[3] SECAM thus studied ways and means of planning a continental meeting of this kind. A consultation of the Episcopal Conferences and of each Bishop of Africa and Madagascar was organized, after which I was able to convoke a Special Assembly for Africa of the Synod of Bishops. On 6 January 1989, the Solemnity of the Epiphany — the liturgical commemoration on which the Church renews her

    [2] Declaration of the Bishops of Africa and Madagascar present at the Third Ordinary General Assembly of the Synod of Bishops (20 October 1974): *La Documentation catholique* 71 (1974), 995-996.
    [3] Address to a group of Bishops of Zaire during their *ad Limina* Visit (21 April 1983), 9: *AAS* 75 (1983), 634-635.

awareness of the universality of her mission and her consequent duty to bring the light of Christ to all peoples — I announced this "initiative of great importance for the Church", welcoming, as I said, the petitions often expressed for some time by the Bishops of Africa, priests, theologians and representatives of the laity, "in order to promote an *organic pastoral solidarity* within the entire African territory and nearby Islands".[4]

An event of grace

6.   The Special Assembly for Africa of the Synod of Bishops was *an historic moment of grace:* the Lord *visited* his people in Africa. Indeed, this Continent is today experiencing what we can call a *sign of the times,* an *acceptable time,* a *day of salvation.* It seems that the "hour of Africa" has come, a favourable time which urgently invites Christ's messengers to launch out into the deep and to cast their nets for the catch (cf. *Lk* 5:4). Just as at Christianity's beginning the minister of Candace, Queen of Ethiopia, rejoiced at having received the faith through Baptism and went on his way bearing witness to Christ (cf. *Acts* 8:27-39), so today the Church in Africa, joyful and grateful for having received the faith, must pursue its evangelizing mission, in order to bring the peoples of the Continent to the Lord, teaching them to observe all that he has commanded (cf. *Mt* 28:20).

From the opening Solemn Eucharistic Liturgy

---

[4] Angelus (6 January 1989), 2: *Insegnamenti* XII/1 (1989), 40.

which on 10 April 1994 I celebrated in Saint Peter's Basilica with thirty-five Cardinals, one Patriarch, thirty-nine Archbishops, one hundred forty-six Bishops and ninety priests, the Church, which is the Family of God [5] and the community of believers, gathered about the Tomb of Peter. Africa was present there, in its various rites, with the entire People of God: it rejoiced, expressing its faith in life to the sound of drums and other African musical instruments. On that occasion Africa felt that it was, in the words of Pope Paul VI, "a new homeland for Christ",[6] a land loved by the Eternal Father.[7] That is why I myself greeted that moment of grace in the words of the Psalmist: "This is the day which the Lord has made; let us rejoice and be glad in it" (*Ps* 118:24).

Recipients of the Exhortation

7. In communion with the Special Assembly for Africa of the Synod of Bishops, I wish to address this Post-Synodal Apostolic Exhortation in the first place to Pastors and lay Catholics, and then to our brothers and sisters of other Christian Confessions, to those who profess the great monotheistic religions, in particular the followers of

---

[5] Cf. SECOND VATICAN ECUMENICAL COUNCIL, Dogmatic Constitution on the Church *Lumen Gentium*, 6.

[6] Homily at the Canonization of Blessed Charles Lwanga, Matthias Molumba Kalemba and Twenty Companion Martyrs (18 October 1964): *AAS* 56 (1964), 907-908.

[7] Cf. JOHN PAUL II, Homily at the Closing Liturgy of the Special Assembly for Africa of the Synod of Bishops (8 May 1994), 6: *L'Osservatore Romano* (English-language edition), 11 May 1994, 2.

African traditional religion, and to all people of good will who in one way or another have at heart Africa's spiritual and material development or who hold in their hands the destiny of this great Continent.

First of all my thoughts naturally turn to the Africans themselves and to all who live on the Continent; I think especially of the sons and daughters of the Catholic Church: Bishops, priests, deacons, seminarians, members of Institutes of Consecrated Life and Societies of Apostolic Life, catechists and all those who make service of their brothers and sisters the ideal of their life. I wish to confirm them in their faith (cf. *Lk* 22:32) and to urge them to persevere in the hope which the Risen Christ gives, overcoming every temptation to discouragement.

Outline of the Exhortation

8. The Special Assembly for Africa of the Synod of Bishops examined thoroughly the topic which had been placed before it: "The Church in Africa and her evangelizing mission towards the Year 2000: 'You shall be my witnesses' (*Acts* 1:8)". This Exhortation will therefore endeavour to follow closely the same thematic framework. It will begin from the historic moment, a true *kairos,* in which the Synod was held, examining its objectives, preparation and celebration. It will consider the current situation of the *Church in Africa,* recalling the different phases of missionary commitment. It will then examine the various aspects of

the *evangelizing* mission which the Church must take into account at the present time: evangelization, inculturation, dialogue, justice and peace, and the means of social communication. A mention of the *urgent tasks* and *challenges* facing the Church in Africa *on the eve of the Year 2000* will enable us to sketch out the tasks of Christ's witnesses in Africa, so that they will make a more effective contribution to the building up of God's Kingdom. It will thus be possible at the end to describe the responsibilities of the Church in Africa as a missionary Church: a Church of mission which itself becomes missionary: "You shall be my witnesses to the ends of the earth" (*Acts* 1:8).

CHAPTER I

AN HISTORIC MOMENT OF GRACE

9. "This Special Assembly for Africa of the Synod of Bishops is a *providential event of grace,* for which we must give praise and thanks to the Almighty and Merciful Father through the Son in the Holy Spirit".[8] It is with these words that the Fathers solemnly opened the discussion of the Synod's theme during the first General Congregation. On an earlier occasion, I had expressed a similar conviction, recognizing that "the Special Assembly is an ecclesial event of fundamental importance for Africa, a *kairos, a moment of grace,* in which God manifests his salvation. The whole Church is invited to live fully this time of grace, to accept and spread the Good News. The effort expended in preparation for the Synod will not only benefit the celebration of the Synod itself, but from this time on will work *in favour of the local Churches which make their pilgrim way in Africa,* whose faith and witness are being strengthened and are becoming increasingly mature".[9]

---

[8] *Relatio ante disceptationem* (11 April 1994), 1: *L'Osservatore Romano,* 13 April 1994, 4.

[9] Address at the Third Meeting of the Council of the General Secretariat for the Special Assembly for Africa of the Synod of Bishops, Luanda (9 June 1992), 5: *AAS* 85 (1993), 523.

10.   This moment of grace was in the first place manifested in a solemn profession of faith. Gathered about the Tomb of Peter for the opening of the Special Assembly, the Synod Fathers proclaimed their faith, the faith of Peter who, in answer to Christ's question, "Do you also wish to go away?", replied: "Lord, to whom shall we go? You have the words of eternal life; and we have believed, and have come to know, that you are the Holy One of God" (*Jn* 6:67-69). The Bishops of Africa, in whom the Catholic Church during those days found herself expressed in a special way at the Tomb of the Apostle, confirmed their steadfast belief that the greatness and mercy of the one God were manifested above all in the Redemptive Incarnation of the Son of God, the Son who is consubstantial with the Father in the unity of the Holy Spirit and who, in this Trinitarian unity, receives the fullness of honour and glory. This — the Fathers affirmed — is our faith; this is the faith of the Church; this is the faith of all the local Churches which everywhere in Africa are on pilgrimage towards the House of God.

This faith in Jesus Christ was manifested unceasingly, forcefully and unanimously in the interventions of the Synod Fathers throughout the meeting of the Special Assembly. In the strength of this faith, the Bishops of Africa entrusted their Continent to Christ the Lord, convinced that he alone, through his Gospel and his Church, can save Africa from its present difficulties and heal its many ills.[10]

11.   At the same time, at the solemn opening of the Special Assembly, the Bishops of Africa publicly proclaimed their faith in the "unique Church of Christ, which in the Creed we avow as one, holy, catholic and apostolic".[11] These characteristics indicate essential features of the Church and her mission. She "does not possess them of herself; it is Christ who, through the Holy Spirit, makes his Church one, holy, catholic and apostolic, and it is he who calls her to realize each of these qualities".[12]

All those privileged to be present at the celebration of the Special Assembly for Africa rejoiced to see how African Catholics are assuming ever greater responsibility in their local Churches and are seeking a deeper understanding of what it means to be both Catholic and African. The celebration of the Special Assembly showed to the whole world that the local Churches of Africa hold a rightful place in the communion of the Church, that they are entitled to preserve and to develop "their own traditions, without in any way lessening the primacy of the Chair of Peter. This Chair presides over the whole assembly of charity and protects legitimate differences, while at the same

    [10] Cf. *Relatio post disceptationem* (22 April 1994), 2: *L'Osservatore Romano*, 24 April 1994, 8.
    [11] SECOND VATICAN ECUMENICAL COUNCIL, Dogmatic Constitution on the Church *Lumen Gentium*, 8.
    [12] *Catechism of the Catholic Church*, No. 811.

time it sees that such differences do not hinder unity but rather contribute towards it".[13]

Synod of Resurrection, Synod of Hope

12.   By a singular design of Providence, the solemn inauguration of the Special Assembly for Africa of the Synod of Bishops took place on the Second Sunday of Easter, at the end of the Easter Octave. The Synod Fathers, assembled in Saint Peter's Basilica on that day, were well aware that the joy of their Church flowed from the same event which had gladdened the Apostles' hearts on Easter Day (cf. *Lk* 24:40-41): the Resurrection of the Lord Jesus. They were deeply aware of the presence in their midst of the Risen Lord, who said to them as he had to his Apostles: "Peace be with you" (*Jn* 20:21,26). They were also aware of his promise to remain with his Church for ever (cf. *Mt* 28:20), and therefore also throughout the duration of the Synodal Assembly. The Easter spirit in which the Special Assembly began its work, with its members united in celebrating their faith in the Risen Lord, spontaneously brought to mind the words which Jesus addressed to the Apostle Thomas: "Blessed are those who have not seen and yet believe" (*Jn* 20:29).

13.   This was indeed a Synod of Resurrection and Hope, as the Synod Fathers joyfully and en- thusiastically declared in the opening words of

[13] SECOND VATICAN ECUMENICAL COUNCIL, Dogmatic Con- stitution on the Church *Lumen Gentium*, 13.

their *Message* to the People of God. They are words which I willingly make my own: "Like Mary Magdalene on the morning of the Resurrection, like the disciples at Emmaus with burning hearts and enlightened minds, the Special Synod for Africa, Madagascar and the Islands proclaims: *Christ, our Hope, is risen. He has met us, has walked along with us.* He has explained the Scriptures to us. Here is what he said to us: 'I am the First and the Last, I am the Living One; I was dead, and behold, I am alive for ever and ever and I hold the keys of death and of the abode of the dead' (*Rev* 1:17-18) ... And as Saint John at Patmos during particularly difficult times received prophecies of hope for the People of God, we also announce a message of hope. At this time when so much fratricidal hate inspired by political interests is tearing our peoples apart, when the burden of the international debt and currency devaluation is crushing them, we, the Bishops of Africa, together with all the participants in this holy Synod, united with the Holy Father and with all our Brothers in the Episcopate who elected us, we want to say a word of hope and encouragement to you, Family of God in Africa, to you, the Family of God all over the world: *Christ our Hope is alive; we shall live!*" [14]

14.   I exhort all God's People in Africa to accept with open hearts the message of hope ad-

[14] *Message of the Synod* (6 May 1994), 1-2: *L'Osservatore Romano* (English-language edition), 11 May 1994, 6.

dressed to them by the Synodal Assembly. During their discussions the Synod Fathers, fully aware that they were expressing the expectations not only of African Catholics but also those of all the men and women of the Continent, squarely faced the many evils which oppress Africa today. The Fathers explored at length and in all its complexity what the Church is called to do in order to bring about the desired changes, but they did so with an attitude free from pessimism or despair. Despite the mainly negative picture which today characterizes numerous parts of Africa, and despite the sad situations being experienced in many countries, the Church has the duty to affirm vigorously that these difficulties can be overcome. She must strengthen in all Africans hope of genuine liberation. In the final analysis, this confidence is based on the Church's awareness of God's promise, which assures us that history is not closed in upon itself but is open to God's Kingdom. This is why there is no justification for despair or pessimism when we think about the future of both Africa and any other part of the world.

Affective and effective collegiality

15.   Before dealing with the different themes, I would like to state that the Synod of Bishops is an extremely beneficial instrument for fostering ecclesial communion. When towards the end of the Second Vatican Council Pope Paul VI established the Synod, he clearly indicated that one of its essential tasks would be to express and foster, under

the guidance of the Successor of Peter, mutual communion between Bishops throughout the world.[15] The principle underlying the setting up of the Synod of Bishops is straightforward: the more the communion of the Bishops among themselves is strengthened, the more the communion of the Church as a whole is enriched. The Church in Africa testifies to the truth of these words, for it has experienced the enthusiasm and practical results which accompanied the preparations for the Assembly of the Synod of Bishops devoted to it.

16.   At my first meeting with the Council of the General Secretariat of the Synod of Bishops, gathered to discuss the Special Assembly for Africa, I indicated the reason why it seemed appropriate to convoke this Assembly: the promotion of "an organic pastoral solidarity throughout Africa and the adjacent Islands".[16] With these words I wished to include the main goals and objectives which that Assembly would have to pursue. In order to clarify my expectations further, I added that the reflections in preparation for the Assembly "should cover all the important aspects of the life of the Church in Africa, and in particular should include evangelization, inculturation, dialogue, pastoral

[15] Cf. Motu Proprio *Apostolica Sollicitudo* (15 September 1965), II: *AAS* 57 (1965), 776-777.

[16] Address to the Council of the General Secretariat for the Special Assembly for Africa of the Synod of Bishops (23 June 1989), 1: *AAS* 82 (1990), 73; cf. Angelus (6 January 1989), 2: *Insegnamenti* XII/1 (1989), 40.

care in social areas and the means of social communication".[17]

17.   During my Pastoral Visits in Africa, I frequently referred to the Special Assembly for Africa and to the principal aims for which it had been convoked. When I took part for the first time on African soil at a meeting of the Council of the Synod, I did not fail to emphasize my conviction that a Synodal Assembly cannot be reduced to a consultation on practical matters. Its true *raison d'être* is the fact that the Church can move forward only by strengthening communion among her members, beginning with her Pastors.[18]

Every Synodal Assembly manifests and develops solidarity between the heads of particular Churches in carrying out their mission beyond the boundaries of their respective Dioceses. The Second Vatican Council taught: "As lawful Successors of the Apostles and as members of the Episcopal College, Bishops should always realize that they are linked one to the other, and should show concern for all the Churches. For by divine institution and the requirement of their apostolic office, each one in concert with his fellow Bishops is responsible for the Church".[19]

---

[17] Address to the Council of the General Secretariat for the Special Assembly for Africa of the Synod of Bishops (23 June 1989), 5: *AAS* 82 (1990), 75.

[18] Cf. Address to the Council of the General Secretariat for the Special Assembly for Africa of the Synod of Bishops, Yamoussoukro (10 September 1990), 3: *AAS* 83 (1991), 226.

[19] Decree on the Bishops' Pastoral Office in the Church *Christus Dominus*, 6.

18

18. The theme assigned to the Special Assembly — "The Church in Africa and her evangelizing mission towards the Year 2000. 'You shall be my witnesses' (*Acts* 1:8)" — expresses my desire that this Church should live the time leading up to the Great Jubilee as "a new Advent", a time of expectation and preparation. In fact I consider preparations for the Year 2000 as one of the keys for interpreting my Pontificate.[20]

The series of Synodal Assemblies which have taken place in the course of nearly thirty years — General Assemblies and Special Assemblies on a continental, regional or national level — are all part of preparing for the Great Jubilee. The fact that evangelization is the theme of all these Synodal Assemblies is meant to indicate how alive today is the Church's awareness of the salvific mission which she has received from Christ. This awareness is especially evident in the Post-Synodal Apostolic Exhortations devoted to evangelization, catechesis, the family, reconciliation and penance in the life of the Church and of all humanity, the vocation and mission of the lay faithful and the formation of priests.

In full communion with the universal Church

19. Right from the beginning of the preparations for the Special Assembly, it was my heartfelt desire, fully shared by the Council of the General

---

[20] Cf. Apostolic Letter *Tertio Millennio Adveniente* (10 November 1994), 23: *AAS* 87 (1995), 19.

Secretariat, to ensure that this Synod would be authentically and unequivocally African. At the same time, it was of fundamental importance that the Special Assembly should be celebrated *in full communion with the universal Church.* Indeed, the Assembly always kept in mind the needs of the universal Church. Likewise, when the time came to publish the *Lineamenta,* I invited my Brothers in the Episcopate and the whole People of God throughout the world to pray for the Special Assembly for Africa, and to feel that they were part of the activities being promoted in preparation for that event.

This Assembly, as I have often had occasion to say, was of profound significance for the universal Church, not only because of the great interest raised everywhere by its convocation, but also because of the very nature of ecclesial communion which transcends all boundaries of time and space. In fact the Special Assembly inspired many prayers and good works through which individuals and communities of the Church in the other continents accompanied the Synodal process. And how can we doubt that through the mystery of ecclesial communion the Synod was also supported by the prayers of the Saints in heaven?

When I directed that the first working session of the Special Assembly should take place in Rome, I did so in order to express even more clearly the communion which links the Church in Africa with the universal Church, and in order to emphasize the commitment of *all the faithful* to Africa.

20. The solemn Eucharistic concelebration for the opening of the Synod at which I presided in Saint Peter's Basilica highlighted the universality of the Church in a striking and deeply moving way. This universality, "which is not uniformity but rather communion in a diversity compatible with the Gospel",[21] was experienced by all the Bishops. They were aware of having been consecrated as members of the Body of Bishops which succeeds the College of the Apostles, not only for one Diocese but for the salvation of the whole world.[22]

I give thanks to Almighty God for the opportunity which he gave us to experience, through the Special Assembly, what genuine catholicity implies. "In virtue of this catholicity each individual part of the Church contributes through its special gifts to the good of the other parts and of the whole Church".[23]

A relevant and credible message

21. According to the Synod Fathers, the main question facing the Church in Africa consists in delineating as clearly as possible what it is and what it must fully carry out, in order that its

---

[21] SYNOD OF BISHOPS, Special Assembly for Africa, *Message of the Synod* (6 May 1994), 7: *L'Osservatore Romano* (English-language edition), 11 May 1994, 6.

[22] Cf. SECOND VATICAN ECUMENICAL COUNCIL, Decree on the Missionary Activity of the Church *Ad Gentes*, 38.

[23] SECOND VATICAN ECUMENICAL COUNCIL, Dogmatic Constitution on the Church *Lumen Gentium*, 13.

message may be relevant and credible.[24] All the discussions at the Assembly referred to this truly essential and fundamental need, which is *a real challenge for the Church in Africa.*

It is of course true "that the Holy Spirit is the principal agent of evangelization: it is he who impels each individual to proclaim the Gospel, and it is he who in the depths of consciences causes the word of salvation to be accepted and understood".[25] After reaffirming this truth, the Special Assembly rightly went on to add that evangelization is also a mission which the Lord Jesus entrusted to his Church under the guidance and in the power of the Holy Spirit. Our cooperation is necessary through fervent prayer, serious reflection, suitable planning and the mobilization of resources.[26]

The Synod's debate on the *relevance* and *credibility* of the Church's message in Africa inescapably entailed consideration of the *very credibility of the proclaimers of this message.* The Synod Fathers faced the question directly, with genuine frankness and devoid of any complacency. Pope Paul VI had already addressed this question in memorable words when he stated: "It is often said nowadays that the present century thirsts for authenticity. Especially in regard to young people, it is said that they have a horror of the artificial or false

---

[24] Cf. *Relatio ante disceptationem* (11 April 1994), 34: *L'Osservatore Romano*, 13 April 1994, 5.

[25] Paul VI, Apostolic Exhortation *Evangelii Nuntiandi* (8 December 1975), 75: *AAS* 68 (1976), 66.

[26] Cf. SYNOD OF BISHOPS, Special Assembly for Africa, *Relatio ante disceptationem*, 34: *L'Osservatore Romano*, 13 April 1994, 5.

and that they are searching above all for truth and honesty. These *signs of the times* should find us vigilant. Either tacitly or aloud — but always forcefully — we are being asked: Do you really believe what you are proclaiming? Do you live what you believe? Do you really preach what you live? The witness of life has become more than ever an essential condition for real effectiveness in preaching. Precisely because of this we are, to a certain extent, responsible for the progress of the Gospel that we proclaim".[27]

That is why, with reference to the Church's evangelizing mission in the field of justice and peace, I have said: "Today more than ever, the Church is aware that her social doctrine will gain credibility more immediately from *witness of action* than as a result of its internal logic and consistency".[28]

22.   How can I fail to recall here that the Eighth Plenary Assembly of SECAM held in Lagos, Nigeria, in 1987, had already considered with remarkable clarity the question of the credibility and relevance of the Church's message in Africa? That same Assembly had declared that the credibility of the Church in Africa depended upon Bishops and priests who followed Christ's example and could give witness of an exemplary life; upon truly faithful men and women religious,

---

[27] Apostolic Exhortation *Evangelii Nuntiandi* (8 December 1975), 76: *AAS* 68 (1976), 67.
[28] Encyclical Letter *Centesimus Annus* (1 May 1991), 57: *AAS* 83 (1991), 862.

authentic witnesses by their way of living the evangelical counsels; upon a dynamic laity, with deeply believing parents, educators conscious of their responsibilities and political leaders animated by a profound sense of morality.[29]

The Family of God in the Synodal process

23.   Speaking to the members of the Council of the General Secretariat on 23 June 1989, I laid special emphasis on the involvement of the whole People of God, at all levels and especially in Africa, in the preparations for the Special Assembly. "If this Synod is prepared well," I said, "it will be able to involve all levels of the Christian Community: individuals, small communities, parishes, Dioceses, and local, national and international bodies".[30]

Between the beginning of my Pontificate and the solemn inauguration of the Special Assembly for Africa of the Synod of Bishops, I paid a total of ten Pastoral Visits to Africa and Madagascar, going to thirty-six countries. On my Apostolic Visits after the convocation of the Special Assembly, the theme of the Synod and the need for all the faithful to prepare for the Synodal Assembly always figured prominently in my meetings with the People of God in Africa. I also took ad-

[29] Cf. Message of the Eighth Plenary Assembly of SECAM (19 July 1987): *La Documentation catholique* 84 (1987), 1024-1026.
[30] Address to the Council of the General Secretariat of the Special Assembly for Africa of the Synod of Bishops (23 June 1989), 6: *AAS* 82 (1990), 76.

vantage of the *ad Limina* Visits of the Continent's Bishops in order to ask for the cooperation of everyone in the preparation of the Special Synod for Africa. In addition, on three separate occasions I held working sessions with the Council of the General Secretariat of the Synod *on African soil:* at Yamoussoukro, Ivory Coast (1990); at Luanda, Angola (1992); and at Kampala, Uganda (1993). All this was done in order to mobilize an active and harmonious participation by Africans in the preparation of the Synodal Assembly.

24. The presentation of the *Lineamenta* at the Ninth Plenary Assembly of SECAM in Lomé, Togo, on 25 July 1990, was undoubtedly a new and significant stage in the preparation of the Special Assembly. It can be said that with the publication of the *Lineamenta* preparations for the Synod began in earnest in all the particular Churches of Africa. The Assembly of SECAM in Lomé approved a *Prayer for the Special Assembly* and requested that it be recited both publicly and privately in every African parish until the actual celebration of the Synod. This initiative of SECAM was truly felicitous and did not pass unnoticed by the universal Church.

In order to make the *Lineamenta* more available, many Episcopal Conferences and Dioceses translated the document into their own languages, for example into Swahili, Arabic, Malagasy, etc. "Publications, conferences and symposia on the themes of the Synod were organized by various Episcopal Conferences, Institutes of Theology and

Seminaries, Associations of Institutes of Consecrated Life, Dioceses, some important journals and periodicals, individual Bishops and theologians".[31]

25. I fervently thank Almighty God for the meticulous care with which the Synod's *Lineamenta* and the *Instrumentum Laboris* [32] were drawn up. It was a task accepted and carried out by Africans — Bishops and experts — beginning with the Ante-Preparatory Commission of the Synod which met in January and March 1989. This Commission was then replaced by the Council of the General Secretariat of the Special Assembly for Africa of the Synod of Bishops, established on 20 June 1989.

I am also deeply grateful to the working group which so carefully prepared the Eucharistic Liturgies for the opening and closing of the Synod. The group, which included theologians, liturgists and experts in African chants and musical instruments, ensured, in keeping with my wishes, that these celebrations would have a distinctly African character.

26. I must now add that the response of the African peoples to my appeal to them to share in

[31] SYNOD OF BISHOPS, Special Assembly for Africa, *Report of the General Secretary* (11 April 1994), VI: *L'Osservatore Romano*, 11-12 April 1994, 10.

[32] Cf. SYNOD OF BISHOPS, Special Assembly for Africa, "The Church in Africa and her Evangelizing Mission Towards the Year 2000: 'You Shall Be my Witnesses' (*Acts* 1:8)": *Lineamenta*, Vatican City, 1990; *Instrumentum Laboris*, Vatican City, 1993.

the preparation of the Synod was truly admirable. The replies given to the *Lineamenta,* both within and beyond the African Ecclesial Communities, far exceeded every expectation. Many local Churches used the *Lineamenta* in order to mobilize the faithful and, from that time onwards, we can say that the results of the Synod were beginning to appear in a fresh commitment and renewed awareness among African Christians.[33]

Throughout the various phases of the preparation for the Special Assembly, many members of the Church in Africa — clergy, religious and laity — entered with exemplary dedication into the Synodal process, "walking together", placing their individual talents at the service of the Church, and fervently praying together for the Synod's success. More than once the Synod Fathers themselves noted, during the actual Synodal Assembly, that their work was made easier precisely by the "careful and meticulous preparation of the Synod, and the active involvement of the entire Church in Africa at all levels".[34]

God wills to save Africa

27.   The Apostle of the Gentiles tells us that God "desires all men to be saved and to come to

---

[33] Cf. *Instrumentum Laboris.* Of the thirty-four Episcopal Conferences in Africa and Madagascar, thirty-one sent in their observations, while the other three were unable to do so because of the difficult situations in which they found themselves.

[34] *Relatio ante disceptationem* (11 April 1994), 1: *L'Osservatore Romano,* 13 April 1994, 4; cf. *Relatio post disceptationem* (22 April 1994), 1: *L'Osservatore Romano,* 24 April 1994, 8.

the knowledge of the truth. For there is one God, and there is one mediator between God and men, the man Christ Jesus, who gave himself as a ransom for all" (1 Tim 2:4-6). Since God, in fact, calls all people to one and the same divine destiny, "we ought to believe that the Holy Spirit in a manner known only to God offers to everyone the possibility of being associated with this Paschal Mystery".[35] God's redeeming love embraces the whole of humanity, every race, tribe and nation: thus it also embraces all the peoples of Africa. Divine Providence willed that Africa should be present during the Passion of Christ in the person of Simon of Cyrene, forced by the Roman soldiers to help the Lord to carry the Cross (cf. Mk 15:21).

28.   The Liturgy of the Sixth Sunday of Easter in 1994, at the Solemn Eucharistic Celebration for the closing of the working session of the Special Assembly, provided me with the occasion to develop a meditation upon God's salvific plan for Africa. One of the Scriptural readings, taken from the Acts of the Apostles, recalled an event which can be understood as *the first step in the Church's mission "ad gentes"*: it is the account of the visit made by Peter, at the bidding of the Holy Spirit, to the home of a Gentile, the centurion Cornelius. Until that time the Gospel had been proclaimed mainly to the Jews. After considerable

---

[35] SECOND VATICAN ECUMENICAL COUNCIL, Pastoral Constitution on the Church in the Modern World *Gaudium et Spes*, 22; cf. *Catechism of the Catholic Church*, No. 1260.

hesitation, Peter, enlightened by the Spirit, decided to go to the house of a Gentile. When he arrived, he discovered to his joyful surprise that the centurion was awaiting Christ and Baptism. The Acts of the Apostles says: "the believers from among the circumcised who came with Peter were amazed, because the gift of the Holy Spirit had been poured out even on the Gentiles. For they heard them speaking in tongues and extolling God" (10:45-46).

In the house of Cornelius the miracle of Pentecost was in a sense repeated. Peter then said: "Truly I perceive that God shows no partiality, but in every nation any one who fears him and does what is right is acceptable to him ... Can anyone forbid water for baptizing these people who have received the Holy Spirit just as we have?" (*Acts* 10:34-35,47).

Thus began the Church's mission *ad gentes,* of which Paul of Tarsus would become the principal herald. The first missionaries who reached the heart of Africa undoubtedly felt an astonishment similar to that experienced by the Christians of the Apostolic age at the outpouring of the Holy Spirit.

29.   God's salvific plan for Africa is at the origin of the growth of the Church on the African Continent. But since by Christ's will the Church is by her nature missionary, it follows that the Church in Africa is itself called to play an active role in God's plan of salvation. For this reason I

have often said that "the Church in Africa is a missionary Church and a mission Church".[36]

The Special Assembly for Africa of the Synod of Bishops had the task of examining appropriate ways and means whereby Africans would be better able to implement the mandate which the Risen Lord gave to his disciples: "Go therefore and make disciples of all nations" (Mt 28:19).

[36] Address at the General Audience (21 August 1985), 3: *Insegnamenti* VIII/2 (1985), 512.

CHAPTER II

THE CHURCH IN AFRICA

I. Brief history
of the continent's evangelization

30. On the opening day of the Special Assembly for Africa of the Synod of Bishops, the first meeting of this kind in history, the Synod Fathers recalled some of the marvels wrought by God in the course of Africa's evangelization. It is a history which goes back to the period of the Church's very birth. The spread of the Gospel has taken place in different phases. The first centuries of Christianity saw the evangelization of Egypt and North Africa. A second phase, involving the parts of the Continent south of the Sahara, took place in the fifteenth and sixteenth centuries. A third phase, marked by an extraordinary missionary effort, began in the nineteenth century.

First phase

31. In a message to the Bishops and to all the peoples of Africa concerning the promotion of the religious, civil and social well-being of the Continent, my venerable Predecessor Paul VI recalled in memorable words the glorious splendour of Africa's Christian past: "We think of the Christian

Churches of Africa whose origins go back to the times of the Apostles and are traditionally associated with the name and teaching of Mark the Evangelist. We think of their countless Saints, Martyrs, Confessors, and Virgins, and recall the fact that from the second to the fourth centuries Christian life in the North of Africa was most vigorous and had a leading place in theological study and literary production. The names of the great doctors and writers come to mind, men like Origen, Saint Athanasius, and Saint Cyril, leaders of the Alexandrian school, and at the other end of the North African coastline, Tertullian, Saint Cyprian and above all Saint Augustine, one of the most brilliant lights of the Christian world. We shall mention the great Saints of the desert, Paul, Anthony, and Pachomius, the first founders of the monastic life, which later spread through their example in both the East and the West. And among many others we want also to mention Saint Frumentius, known by the name of Abba Salama, who was consecrated Bishop by Saint Athanasius and became the first Apostle of Ethiopia".[37] During these first centuries of the Church in Africa, certain women also bore their own witness to Christ. Among them Saints Perpetua and Felicitas, Saint Monica and Saint Thecla are particularly deserving of mention.

"These noble examples, as also the saintly African Popes, Victor I, Melchiades and Gelasius

---

[37] Message *Africae Terrarum* (29 October 1967), 3: *AAS* 59 (1967), 1074-1075.

I, belong to the common heritage of the Church, and the Christian writers of Africa remain today a basic source for deepening our knowledge of the history of salvation in the light of the Word of God. In recalling the ancient glories of Christian Africa, we wish to express our profound respect for the Churches with which we are not in full communion: the Greek Church of the Patriarchate of Alexandria, the Coptic Church of Egypt and the Church of Ethiopia, which share with the Catholic Church a common origin and the doctrinal and spiritual heritage of the great Fathers and Saints, not only of their own land, but of all the early Church. They have laboured much and suffered much to keep the Christian name alive in Africa through all the vicissitudes of history".[38] These Churches continue to give evidence down to our own times of the Christian vitality which flows from their Apostolic origins. This is especially true in Egypt, in Ethiopia and, until the seventeenth century, in Nubia. At that time a new phase of evangelization was beginning on the rest of the Continent.

Second phase

32.   In the fifteenth and sixteenth centuries, the exploration of the African coast by the Portuguese was soon accompanied by the evangelization of the regions of Sub-Saharan Africa. That endeavour included the regions of present-day

[38] *Ibid.*, 3-4: *loc. cit.*, 1075.

Benin, São Tomé, Angola, Mozambique and Madagascar.

On Pentecost Sunday, 7 June 1992, for the commemoration of the five hundred years of the evangelization of Angola, I said in Luanda: "The Acts of the Apostles indicate by name the inhabitants of the places who participated directly in the birth of the Church and the work of the breath of the Holy Spirit. They all said: 'We hear them telling in our own tongues the mighty works of God' (*Acts* 2:11). Five hundred years ago the people of Angola were added to this chorus of languages. In that moment, in your African homeland the Pentecost of Jerusalem was renewed. Your ancestors heard the message of the Good News which is the language of the Spirit. Their hearts accepted this message for the first time, and they bowed their heads to the waters of the baptismal font in which, by the power of the Holy Spirit, a person dies with Christ and is born again to new life in his Resurrection ... It was certainly the same Spirit who moved those men of faith, the first missionaries, who in 1491 sailed into the mouth of the Zaire River, at Pinda, beginning a genuine missionary saga. It was the Holy Spirit, who works as he wills in people's hearts, who moved the great King of the Congo, Nzinga-a-Nkuwu, to ask for missionaries to proclaim the Gospel. It was the Holy Spirit who sustained the life of those four first Angolan Christians who, returning from Europe, testified to the Christian faith. After the first missionaries, many others came from Portugal and other

European countries to continue, expand and strengthen the work that had been begun".[39]

A certain number of Episcopal Sees were erected during this period, and one of the first fruits of that missionary endeavour was the consecration in Rome, by Pope Leo X in 1518, of Don Henrique, the son of Don Alfonso I, King of the Congo, as Titular Bishop of Utica. Don Henrique thus became the first native Bishop of Black Africa.

It was during this period, in 1622, that my Predecessor Pope Gregory XV permanently erected the Congregation *de Propaganda Fide* for the purpose of better organizing and expanding the missions.

Because of various difficulties, the second phase of the evangelization of Africa came to an end in the eighteenth century, with the disappearance of practically all the missions south of the Sahara.

Third phase

33. The third phase of Africa's systematic evangelization began in the nineteenth century, a period marked by an extraordinary effort organized by the great apostles and promoters of the African mission. It was a period of rapid growth, as the statistics presented to the Synodal Assembly by the Congregation for the Evangelization of

[39] Homily at the Mass commemorating the Five Hundredth Anniversary of Evangelization in Angola, Luanda (7 June 1992), 2: *AAS* 85 (1993), 511-512.

Peoples clearly demonstrate.[40] Africa has responded with great generosity to Christ's call. In recent decades many African countries have celebrated the first centenary of the beginning of their evangelization. Indeed, the growth of the Church in Africa over the last hundred years is a marvellous work of divine grace.

The glory and splendour of the present period of Africa's evangelization are illustrated in a truly admirable way by the Saints whom modern Africa has given to the Church. Pope Paul VI eloquently expressed this when he canonized the Ugandan Martyrs in Saint Peter's Basilica on World Mission Day, 1964: "These African Martyrs add a new page to that list of victorious men and women that we call the martyrology, in which we find the most magnificent as well as the most tragic stories. The page that they add is worthy to take its place alongside those wonderful stories of ancient Africa ... For from the Africa that was sprinkled with the blood of these Martyrs, the first of this new age (and, God willing, the last, so sublime, so precious was their sacrifice), there is emerging a free and redeemed Africa".[41]

34. The list of Saints that Africa gives to the Church, the list that is its greatest title of honour,

[40] Cf. "Situation of the Church in Africa and Madagascar: Some Factors and Observations", L'Osservatore Romano, 16 April 1994, 6-8; OFFICE OF CHURCH STATISTICS, "The Church in Africa: Numbers and Statistics (1978-1992)", L'Osservatore Romano, 15 April 1994, 6.

[41] Homily for the Canonization of Blessed Charles Lwanga, Matthias Molumba Kalemba and Twenty Companion Martyrs (18 October 1964): AAS 56 (1964), 905-906.

continues to grow. How could we fail to mention, among the most recent, Blessed Clementine Anwarite, Virgin and Martyr of Zaire, whom I beatified on African soil in 1985, Blessed Victoria Rasoamanarivo of Madagascar, and Blessed Josephine Bakhita of the Sudan, also beatified during my Pontificate? And how can we not recall Blessed Isidore Bakanja, Martyr of Zaire, whom I had the privilege of raising to the honours of the altar in the course of the Special Assembly for Africa? "Other causes are reaching their final stages. *The Church in Africa must furnish and write her own Martyrology,* adding to the outstanding figures of the first centuries ... the Martyrs and Saints of our own day".[42]

Faced with the tremendous growth of the Church in Africa over the last hundred years and the fruits of holiness that it has borne, there is only one possible explanation: all this is a gift of God, for no human effort alone could have performed this work in the course of such a relatively short period of time. There is however no reason for worldly triumphalism. In recalling the glorious splendour of the Church in Africa, the Synod Fathers only wished to celebrate God's marvellous deeds for Africa's liberation and salvation.

"This is the Lord's doing;
    it is marvellous in our eyes" (*Ps* 118:23).
"He who is mighty has done great things for
    me, and holy is his name" (*Lk* 1:49).

[42] JOHN PAUL II, Homily for the closing celebration of the Special Assembly for Africa of the Synod of Bishops (8 May 1994), 6: *L'Osservatore Romano* (English-language edition), 11 May 1994, 2.

35.   The splendid growth and achievements of
the Church in Africa are due largely to the heroic
and selfless dedication of generations of missionaries. This fact is acknowledged by everyone. The
hallowed soil of Africa is truly sown with the
tombs of courageous heralds of the Gospel.

When the Bishops of Africa met in Rome for
the Special Assembly, they were well aware of the
debt of gratitude which their Continent owes to
its ancestors in the faith.

In his Address to the inaugural Assembly of
SECAM at Kampala, on 31 July 1969, Pope Paul
VI spoke about this debt of gratitude: "By now,
you Africans are missionaries to yourselves. The
Church of Christ is well and truly planted in this
blessed soil (cf. *Ad Gentes,* 6). One duty, however, remains to be fulfilled: we must remember
those who, before you, and even today with you,
have preached the Gospel in Africa; for Sacred
Scripture admonishes us to 'Remember your leaders, those who spoke to you the word of God;
consider the outcome of their life; and imitate
their faith' (*Heb* 13:7). That is a history which we
must not forget; it confers on the local Church the
mark of its authenticity and nobility, its mark as
'apostolic'. That history is a drama of charity,
heroism and sacrifice which makes the African
Church great and holy from its very origins".[43]

---

[43] Address to the Symposium of Episcopal Conferences of
Africa and Madagascar, Kampala (31 July 1969), 1: *AAS* 61 (1969),
575.

36.   The Special Assembly worthily fulfilled this debt of gratitude at its first General Congregation when it declared: "It is appropriate at this point to pay profound homage to the *missionaries,* men and women of all the Religious and Secular Institutes, as well as to all the countries which, during the almost two thousand years of the evangelization of the African Continent, devoted themselves, without counting the cost, to the task of transmitting the torch of the Christian faith ... That is why we, the happy inheritors of this marvellous adventure, joyfully pay our debt of thanks to God on this solemn occasion".[44]

The Synod Fathers strongly reiterated their homage to the missionaries in their *Message* to the People of God, but they did not forget to pay tribute to the sons and daughters of Africa who served as co-workers of the missionaries, especially catechists and translators.[45]

37.   It is thanks to the great missionary epic which took place on the African Continent, especially during the last two centuries, that we were able to meet in Rome in order to celebrate the Special Assembly for Africa. The seed sown at that time has borne much fruit. My Brothers in the Episcopate, who are sons of the peoples of Africa, are eloquent witnesses to this. Together with their priests, they now carry on their shoul-

---

[44] *Relatio ante disceptationem* (11 April 1994), 5: *L'Osservatore Romano,* 13 April 1994, 4.

[45] Cf. No. 10: *L'Osservatore Romano* (English-language edition), 11 May 1994, 6.

ders the major part of the work of evangelization. Signs of this fruitfulness are also the many sons and daughters of Africa who enter the older missionary Congregations or the new Institutes founded on African soil, taking into their own hands the torch of total consecration to the service of God and the Gospel.

Deeper roots and growth of the Church

38.   The fact that in the course of almost two centuries the number of African Catholics has grown quickly is an outstanding achievement by any standard. In particular, the building up of the Church on the Continent is confirmed by facts such as the noteworthy and rapid increase in the number of ecclesiastical circumscriptions, the growth of a native clergy, of seminarians and candidates for Institutes of Consecrated Life, and the steady increase in the network of catechists, whose contribution to the spread of the Gospel among the African peoples is well known. Finally, of fundamental importance is the high percentage of indigenous Bishops who now make up the Hierarchy on the Continent.

The Synod Fathers identified many very significant accomplishments of the Church in Africa in the areas of inculturation and ecumenical dialogue.[46] The outstanding and meritorious achievements in the field of education are universally acknowledged.

---

[46] Cf. *Relatio post disceptationem* (22 April 1994), 22-26: *L'Osservatore Romano*, 24 April 1994, 8.

Although Catholics constitute only fourteen per cent of the population of Africa, Catholic health facilities make up seventeen per cent of the health-care institutions of the entire Continent.

The initiatives boldly undertaken by the young Churches of Africa in order to bring the Gospel "to the ends of the earth" (*Acts* 1:8) are certainly worthy of note. The missionary Institutes founded in Africa have grown in number, and have begun to supply missionaries not only for the countries of the Continent but also for other areas of the world. A slowly increasing number of African diocesan priests are beginning to make themselves available, for limited periods, as *fidei donum* priests in other needy Dioceses — in their own countries or abroad. The African provinces of Religious Institutes of pontifical right, both of men and of women, have also recorded a growth in membership. In this way the Church offers her ministry to the peoples of Africa; but she also accepts involvement in the "exchange of gifts" with other particular Churches which make up the People of God. All this manifests, in a tangible way, the maturity which the Church in Africa has attained: this is what made possible the celebration of the Special Assembly of the Synod of Bishops.

What has become of Africa?

39.   A little less than thirty years ago many African countries gained their independence from the colonial powers. This gave rise to great hopes with

regard to the political, economic, social and cultural development of the African peoples. However, "in some countries the internal situation has unfortunately not yet been consolidated, and violence has had, or in some cases still has, the upper hand. But this does not justify a general condemnation involving a whole people or a whole nation or, even worse, a whole continent".[47]

40.   But what is the true overall situation of the African Continent today, especially from the point of view of the Church's evangelizing mission? In this regard the Synod Fathers first of all asked: "In a Continent full of bad news, how is the Christian message 'Good News' for our people? In the midst of an all-pervading despair, where lie the hope and optimism which the Gospel brings? Evangelization stands for many of those essential values which our Continent very much lacks: hope, peace, joy, harmony, love and unity".[48]

After correctly noting that Africa is a huge Continent where very diverse situations are found, and that it is necessary to avoid generalizations both in evaluating problems and suggesting solutions, the Synodal Assembly sadly had to say: "One common situation, without any doubt, is that Africa is full of problems. In almost all our nations, there is abject poverty, tragic mismanagement of available scarce resources, political in-

---

[47] Paul VI, Message *Africae Terrarum* (29 October 1967), 6: *AAS* 59 (1967), 1076.
[48] *Relatio ante disceptationem* (11 April 1994), 2: *L'Osservatore Romano*, 13 April 1994, 4.

stability and social disorientation. The results stare us in the face: misery, wars, despair. In a world controlled by rich and powerful nations, Africa has practically become an irrelevant appendix, often forgotten and neglected".[49]

41. For many Synod Fathers contemporary Africa can be compared to the man who went down from Jerusalem to Jericho; he fell among robbers who stripped him, beat him and departed, leaving him half dead (cf. *Lk* 10:30-37). Africa is a Continent where countless human beings — men and women, children and young people — are lying, as it were, on the edge of the road, sick, injured, disabled, marginalized and abandoned. They are in dire need of Good Samaritans who will come to their aid.

For my part, I express the hope that the Church will continue patiently and tirelessly its work as a Good Samaritan. Indeed, for a long period certain regimes, which have now come to an end, were a great trial for Africans and weakened their ability to respond to situations: an injured person has to rediscover all the resources of his own humanity. The sons and daughters of Africa need an understanding presence and pastoral concern. They need to be helped to recoup their energies so as to put them at the service of the common good.

---

[49] *Ibid.*, 4: *loc. cit.*

42.   Although Africa is very rich in natural resources, it remains economically poor. At the same
time, it is endowed with a wealth of cultural values
and priceless human qualities which it can offer to
the Churches and to humanity as a whole. The
Synod Fathers highlighted some of these cultural
values, which are truly a providential preparation
for the transmission of the Gospel. They are values which can contribute to an effective reversal
of the Continent's dramatic situation and facilitate
that worldwide revival on which the desired development of individual nations depends.

Africans have a profound religious sense, a
sense of the sacred, of the existence of God the
Creator and of a spiritual world. The reality of sin
in its individual and social forms is very much
present in the consciousness of these peoples, as is
also the need for rites of purification and
expiation.

43.   In African culture and tradition the role of
the family is everywhere held to be fundamental.
Open to this sense of the family, of love and respect for life, the African loves children, who are
joyfully welcomed as gifts of God. *"The sons and
daughters of Africa love life.* It is precisely this love
for life that leads them to give such great importance to the veneration of their ancestors. They
believe intuitively that the dead continue to live
and remain in communion with them. Is this not
in some way *a preparation for belief in the Commu-*

nion of the Saints? The peoples of Africa respect the life which is conceived and born. They rejoice in this life. They reject the idea that it can be destroyed, even when the so-called 'progressive civilizations' would like to lead them in this direction. And practices hostile to life are imposed on them by means of economic systems which serve the selfishness of the rich".[50] Africans show their respect for human life until its natural end, and keep elderly parents and relatives within the family.

African cultures have an acute sense of solidarity and community life. In Africa it is unthinkable to celebrate a feast without the participation of the whole village. Indeed, community life in African societies expresses the extended family. It is my ardent hope and prayer that Africa will always preserve this priceless cultural heritage and never succumb to the temptation to individualism, which is so alien to its best traditions.

Some choices of the African peoples

44.   While the shadows and the dark side of the African situation described above can in no way be minimized, it is worth recalling here a number of positive achievements of the peoples of the Continent which deserve to be praised and encouraged. For example, the Synod Fathers in their *Message* to the People of God were pleased to mention the beginning of the democratic process

[50] JOHN PAUL II, Homily at the Opening Liturgy of the Special Assembly for Africa of the Synod of Bishops (10 April 1994), 3: *AAS* 87 (1995), 180-181.

in many African countries, expressing the hope that this process would be consolidated, and that all obstacles and resistance to the establishment of the rule of law would be promptly removed through the concerted action of all those involved and through their sense of the common good.[51]

The "winds of change" are blowing strongly in many parts of Africa, and people are demanding ever more insistently the recognition and promotion of human rights and freedoms. In this regard I note with satisfaction that the Church in Africa, faithful to its vocation, stands resolutely on the side of the oppressed and of voiceless and marginalized peoples. I strongly encourage it to continue to bear this witness. *The preferential option for the poor* is "a special form of primacy in the exercise of Christian charity, to which the whole Tradition of the Church bears witness ... The motivating concern for the poor — who are in the very meaning of the term 'the Lord's poor' — must be translated at all levels into concrete actions, until it decisively attains a series of necessary reforms".[52]

45. In spite of its poverty and the meagre means at its disposal, the Church in Africa plays a leading role in what touches upon integral human development. Its remarkable achievements in this regard are often recognized by governments and international experts.

---

[51] Cf. No. 36: *L'Osservatore Romano*, 11 May 1994, 8.
[52] JOHN PAUL II, Encyclical Letter *Sollicitudo Rei Socialis* (30 December 1987), 42-43: *AAS* 80 (1988), 572-574.

The Special Assembly for Africa expressed deep gratitude "to all Christians and to all men and women of good will who are working in the fields of assistance and health-care with *Caritas* and other development organizations".[53] The assistance which they, as Good Samaritans, give to the African victims of wars and disasters, to refugees and displaced persons, deserves the admiration, gratitude and support of all.

I feel it my duty to express heartfelt thanks to the Church in Africa for the role which it has played over the years as a promoter of peace and reconciliation in many situations of conflict, political turmoil and civil war.

II. PRESENT-DAY PROBLEMS
OF THE CHURCH IN AFRICA

46. The Bishops of Africa are faced with two fundamental questions. How must the Church carry out her evangelizing mission as the Year 2000 approaches? How can African Christians become ever more faithful witnesses to the Lord Jesus? In order to provide adequate responses to these questions the Bishops, both before and during the Special Assembly, examined the major challenges that the Ecclesial Community in Africa must face today.

---

[53] *Message of the Synod* (6 May 1994), 39: *L'Osservatore Romano* (English-language edition), 11 May 1994, 8.

47.   The primary and most fundamental fact noted by the Synod Fathers is the thirst for God felt by the peoples of Africa. In order not to disappoint this expectation, the members of the Church must first of all deepen their faith.[54] Indeed, precisely because she evangelizes, the Church must "begin by being evangelized herself".[55] She needs to meet the challenge raised by "this theme of the Church which is evangelized by constant conversion and renewal, in order to evangelize the world with credibility".[56]

The Synod recognized the urgency of proclaiming the Good News to the millions of people in Africa who are not yet evangelized. The Church certainly respects and esteems the non-Christian religions professed by very many Africans, for these religions are the living expression of the soul of vast groups of people. However, "neither respect and esteem for these religions nor the complexity of the questions raised is an invitation to the Church to withhold from these non-Christians the proclamation of Jesus Christ. On the contrary the Church holds that these multitudes have the right to know the riches of the mystery of Christ (cf. *Eph* 3:8) — riches in which we believe that the whole of humanity can find, in unsuspected

---

[54] Cf. SYNOD OF BISHOPS, Special Assembly for Africa, *Relatio ante disceptationem* (11 April 1994), 6: *L'Osservatore Romano*, 13 April 1994, 4.

[55] PAUL VI, Apostolic Exhortation *Evangelii Nuntiandi* (8 December 1975), 15: *AAS* 68 (1976), 14.

[56] *Ibid.: loc. cit.*, 15.

fullness, everything that it is gropingly searching for concerning God, man and his destiny, life and death, and truth".[57]

48.   The Synod Fathers rightly affirmed that "a serious concern for a true and balanced incultura- tion is necessary in order to avoid cultural confu- sion and alienation in our fast evolving society".[58] During my visit to Malawi I made the same point: *"I put before you today a challenge* — a challenge to reject a way of living which does not correspond to the best of your traditions, and your Christian faith. Many people in Africa look beyond Africa for the so-called 'freedom of the modern way of life'. Today I urge you *to look inside yourselves. Look to the riches of your own traditions, look to the faith* which we are celebrating in this assembly. Here you will find genuine freedom — here you will find Christ who will lead you to the truth".[59]

Overcoming divisions

49.   Another challenge identified by the Synod Fathers concerns the various forms of division which need to be healed through honest dialogue.[60] It has been rightly noted that, within the borders left behind by the colonial powers, the co-exis-

---

[57] *Ibid.*, 53: *loc. cit.*, 42.
[58] *Relatio ante disceptationem*, (11 April 1994), 6: *L'Osservatore Romano*, 13 April 1994, 4.
[59] Homily at the conclusion of the sixth Pastoral Visit in Africa, Li- longwe (6 May 1989), 6: *Insegnamenti* XII/1 (1989), 1183.
[60] Cf. *Relatio ante disceptationem* (11 April 1994), 6: *L'Osservatore Romano*, 13 April 1994, 4.

tence of ethnic groups with different traditions, languages, and even religions often meets obstacles arising from serious mutual hostility. *"Tribal oppositions* at times endanger if not peace, at least the pursuit of the common good of the society. They also create difficulties for the life of the Churches and the acceptance of Pastors from other ethnic groups".[61] This is why the Church in Africa feels challenged by the specific responsibility of healing these divisions. For the same reason the Special Assembly emphasized the importance of ecumenical dialogue with other Churches and Ecclesial Communities, and of dialogue with African traditional religion and Islam. The Fathers also considered the means to be used to achieve this goal.

Marriage and vocations

50. A major challenge emphasized almost unanimously by the Episcopal Conferences of Africa in their replies to the *Lineamenta* concerned Christian marriage and family life.[62] What is at stake is extremely serious: truly "the future of the world and of the Church passes through the family".[63]

---

[61] PONTIFICAL COMMISSION "IUSTITIA ET PAX", *The Church and Racism: Towards a More Fraternal Society* (3 November 1988), 12: Vatican City, 1988.

[62] Cf. SYNOD OF BISHOPS, Special Assembly for Africa, *Instrumentum Laboris*, 68; *Relatio ante disceptationem* (11 April 1994), 17: *L'Osservatore Romano*, 13 April 1994, 5; *Relatio post disceptationem* (22 April 1994), 6, 9, 21: *L'Osservatore Romano*, 24 April 1994, 8.

[63] JOHN PAUL II, Apostolic Exhortation *Familiaris Consortio* (22 November 1981), 75: *AAS* 74 (1982), 173.

Another fundamental responsibility which the Special Assembly highlighted is concern for vocations to the priesthood and consecrated life. It is necessary to discern them wisely, to provide competent directors and to oversee the quality of the formation offered. The fulfilment of the hope for a flowering of African missionary vocations depends on the attention given to the solution of this problem, a flowering that is required if the Gospel is to be proclaimed in every part of the Continent and beyond.

Social and political difficulties

51.   "In Africa, the need to apply the Gospel to concrete life is felt strongly. How could one proclaim Christ on that immense Continent while forgetting that it is one of the world's poorest regions? How could one fail to take into account the anguished history of a land where many nations are still in the grip of famine, war, racial and tribal tensions, political instability and the violation of human rights? This is all a challenge to evangelization". [64]

All the preparatory documents of the Synod, as well as the discussions in the Assembly, clearly showed that issues in Africa such as increasing poverty, urbanization, the international debt, the arms trade, the problem of refugees and displaced persons, demographic concerns and threats to the

[64] JOHN PAUL II, Angelus (20 March 1994), 1: *L'Osservatore Romano* (English-language edition), 23 March 1994, 1.

51

family, the liberation of women, the spread of AIDS, the survival of the practice of slavery in some places, ethnocentricity and tribal opposition figure among the fundamental challenges addressed by the Synod.

Intrusiveness of the mass media

52.   Finally, the Special Assembly addressed the means of social communication, an issue which is of the greatest importance because it concerns both the instruments of evangelization and the means of spreading a new culture which needs to be evangelized.[65] The Synod Fathers were thus faced with the sad fact that "the developing nations, instead of becoming *autonomous nations* concerned with their own progress towards a just sharing in the goods and services meant for all, become parts of a machine, cogs on a gigantic wheel. This is often true also in the field of social communications which, being run by centres mostly in the northern hemisphere, do not always give due consideration to the priorities and problems of such countries or respect their cultural make-up. They frequently impose a distorted vision of life and of man, and thus fail to respond to the demands of true development".[66]

[65] Cf. SYNOD OF BISHOPS, Special Assembly for Africa, *Message of the Synod* (6 May 1994), 45-47: *L'Osservatore Romano* (English-language edition), 11 May 1994, 8.

[66] JOHN PAUL II, Encyclical Letter *Sollicitudo Rei Socialis* (30 December 1987), 22: *AAS* 80 (1988), 539.

III. FORMATION OF THE AGENTS
OF EVANGELIZATION

53.   With what resources will the Church in Africa succeed in meeting the challenges just mentioned? "The most important [resource], after the grace of Christ, is the people. The whole People of God in the theological understanding of *Lumen Gentium* — this People, which comprises the members of the Body of Christ in its entirety — has received the mandate, which is both an honour and a duty, to proclaim the Gospel ... The whole community needs to be trained, motivated and empowered for evangelization, each according to his or her specific role within the Church".[67] For this reason the Synod strongly emphasized the training of the agents of evangelization in Africa. I have already referred to the necessity of formation for candidates to the priesthood and those called to the consecrated life. The Assembly also paid due attention to the formation of the lay faithful, appropriately recognizing their indispensable role in the evangelization of Africa. In particular, the training of lay catechists received the emphasis which it rightly deserves.

54.   A last question must be asked: Has the Church in Africa sufficiently formed the lay faithful, enabling them to assume competently their civic responsibilities and to consider socio-political

---

[67] SYNOD OF BISHOPS, Special Assembly for Africa, *Relatio ante disceptationem* (11 April 1994), 8: *L'Osservatore Romano*, 13 April 1994, 4.

problems in the light of the Gospel and of faith in God? This is certainly a task belonging to Christians: to bring to bear upon the social fabric an influence aimed at changing not only ways of thinking but also the very structures of society, so that they will better reflect God's plan for the human family. Consequently I have called for the thorough formation of the lay faithful, a formation which will help them to lead a fully integrated life. Faith, hope and charity must influence the actions of the true follower of Christ in every activity, situation and responsibility. Since "evangelizing means bringing the Good News into all the strata of humanity, and through its influence transforming humanity from within and making it new",[68] Christians must be formed to live the social implications of the Gospel in such a way that their witness will become a prophetic challenge to whatever hinders the true good of the men and women of Africa and of every other continent.

[68] PAUL VI, Apostolic Exhortation *Evangelii Nuntiandi* (8 December 1975), 18: *AAS* 68 (1976), 17.

CHAPTER III

EVANGELIZATION AND INCULTURATION

The Church's mission

55. "Go into all the world and preach the Gospel to the whole creation" (*Mk* 16:15). Such is the mandate that the Risen Christ, before returning to his Father, gave to his Apostles: "And they went forth and preached everywhere" (*Mk* 16:20).

"The task of evangelizing all people constitutes the essential mission of the Church ... Evangelizing is in fact *the grace and vocation proper to the Church,* her deepest identity. She *exists in order to evangelize*".[69] Born of the evangelizing mission of Jesus and the Twelve, she is in turn sent forth. "Depositary of the Good News to be proclaimed ... having been sent and evangelized, the Church herself sends out evangelizers. She puts on their lips the saving Word".[70] Like the Apostle to the Gentiles, the Church can say: "I preach the Gospel ... For necessity is laid upon me. Woe to me if I do not preach the Gospel!" (*1 Cor* 9:16).

The Church proclaims the Good News of Christ not only by the *proclamation of the Word* which she has received from the Lord, but also by

---

[69] PAUL VI, Apostolic Exhortation *Evangelii Nuntiandi* (8 December 1975), 14: *AAS* 68 (1976), 13.

[70] *Ibid.,* 15: *loc. cit.,* 15.

the *witness of life,* thanks to which Christ's disciples bear witness to the faith, hope and love which dwell in them (cf. *1 Pet* 2:15).

This testimony which the Christian bears to Christ and the Gospel can lead even to the supreme sacrifice: martyrdom (cf. *Mk* 8:35). For the Church and the Christian proclaim the One who is "a sign of contradiction" (cf. *Lk* 2:34). They preach "Christ crucified, a stumbling block to Jews and folly to Gentiles" (*1 Cor* 1:23). As I said earlier, besides honouring the illustrious Martyrs of the first centuries, Africa can glory in its Martyrs and Saints of the modern age.

The purpose of evangelization is "transforming humanity from within and making it new".[71] In and through the Only Son the relations of people with God, one another and all creation will be renewed. For this reason the proclamation of the Gospel can contribute to the interior transformation of all people of good will whose hearts are open to the Holy Spirit's action.

56.   To bear witness to the Gospel in word and deed: this is the task which the Special Assembly for Africa of the Synod of Bishops received and which it now passes on to the Church of the Continent. "You shall be my witnesses" (*Acts* 1:8): this is the challenge. In Africa these should be the fruits of the Synod in every area of people's lives.

Born of the preaching of valiant missionary Bishops and priests, effectively assisted by "the

[71] *Ibid.,* 18: *loc. cit.,* 17.

ranks of men and women catechists, to whom missionary work among the nations owes so very much",[72] the Church in Africa, having become "a new homeland for Christ",[73] is now responsible for the evangelization of the Continent and the world. As my Predecessor Pope Paul VI said in Kampala: "Africans, you are now your own missionaries".[74] Because the vast majority of Africans have not yet heard the Good News of salvation, the Synod recommends that missionary vocations should be encouraged and asks that prayer, sacrifice and effective solidarity for the Church's missionary work be favoured and actively supported.[75]

Proclamation

57. "The Synod recalls that to evangelize is to proclaim by word and witness of life the Good News of Jesus Christ, crucified, died and risen, the Way, the Truth and the Life".[76] To Africa, which is menaced on all sides by outbreaks of hatred and violence, by conflicts and wars, evangelizers must proclaim *the hope of life rooted in the Paschal Mystery*. It was precisely when, humanly speaking, Jesus' life seemed doomed to failure

---

[72] SECOND VATICAN ECUMENICAL COUNCIL, Decree on the Missionary Activity of the Church *Ad Gentes*, 17.

[73] PAUL VI, Homily at the Canonization of Blessed Charles Lwanga, Matthias Molumba Kalemba and Twenty Companion Martyrs (18 October 1964): *AAS* 56 (1964), 907-908.

[74] Address to the Symposium of Episcopal Conferences of Africa and Madagascar, Kampala (31 July 1969), 1: *AAS* 61 (1969), 575; cf. *Propositio* 10.

[75] Cf. *Propositio* 10.

[76] *Propositio* 3.

that he instituted the Eucharist, "the pledge of eternal glory",[77] in order to perpetuate in time and space his victory over death. That is why at a time when the African Continent is in some ways in a critical situation the Special Assembly for Africa wished to be "the *Synod of Resurrection, the Synod of Hope ... Christ our Hope is alive; we shall live!*"[78] Africa is not destined for death, but for life!

It is therefore essential that "the new evangelization should be centred on a transforming encounter with *the living person of Christ*".[79] "The first proclamation ought to bring about this overwhelming and exhilarating experience of Jesus Christ who calls each one to follow him in an adventure of faith".[80] This task is made all the easier because "the African believes in God the Creator from his traditional life and religion and thus is also open to the full and definitive revelation of God in Jesus Christ, God with us, Word made flesh. Jesus, the Good News, is God who saves the African ... from oppression and slavery".[81]

Evangelization must reach "individual human beings and society in every aspect of their existence. It is therefore expressed in various activities, and particularly in those which the Synod examined: proclamation, inculturation, dialogue,

[77] Antiphon *O sacrum convivium:* Magnificat at Second Vespers for the Solemnity of the Body and Blood of Christ.
[78] *Message of the Synod* (6 May 1994), 2: *L'Osservatore Romano* (English-language edition), 11 May 1994, 6.
[79] *Propositio* 4.
[80] SYNOD OF BISHOPS, Special Assembly for Africa, *Message of the Synod* (6 May 1994), 9: *L'Osservatore Romano* (English-language edition), 11 May 1994, 6.
[81] *Propositio* 4.

justice and peace and the means of social communication".[82]

For the full success of this mission, it must be ensured that "in evangelization prayer to the Holy Spirit will be stressed for a continuing Pentecost, where Mary, as at the first Pentecost, will have her place".[83] The power of the Holy Spirit guides the Church into all truth (cf. *Jn* 16:13), enabling her to go into the world in order to bear witness to Christ with confident resolve.

58.   The Word that comes from the mouth of God is living and active, and never returns to him in vain (cf. *Is* 55:11; *Heb* 4:12-13). We must therefore proclaim that Word tirelessly, exhorting "in season and out of season ... unfailing in patience and in teaching" (2 *Tim* 4:2). Entrusted first of all to the Church, the written Word of God is not "a matter of one's own interpretation" (2 *Pet* 1:20), but is to be authentically interpreted by the Church.[84]

In order that the Word of God may be known, loved, pondered and preserved in the hearts of the faithful (cf. *Lk* 2:19,51), greater efforts must be made to provide access to the Sacred Scriptures, especially through full or partial translations of the Bible, prepared as far as possible in cooperation with other Churches and Ecclesial Communities and accompanied by study-guides for use in prayer and for study in the

[82] *Propositio* 3.
[83] *Propositio* 4.
[84] Cf. *Propositio* 6.

family and community. Also to be encouraged is the scriptural formation of clergy, religious, catechists and the laity in general; careful preparation of celebrations of the Word; promotion of the biblical apostolate with the help of the Biblical Centre for Africa and Madagascar and the encouragement of other similar structures at all levels. In brief, efforts must be made to try to put the Sacred Scriptures into the hands of all the faithful right from their earliest years.[85]

Urgent need for inculturation

59.   On several occasions the Synod Fathers stressed the particular importance for evangelization of inculturation, the process by which "catechesis *'takes flesh'* in the various cultures".[86] Inculturation includes two dimensions: on the one hand, "the intimate transformation of authentic cultural values through their integration in Christianity" and, on the other, "the insertion of Christianity in the various human cultures".[87] The Synod considers inculturation an urgent priority in the life of the particular Churches, for a firm rooting of the Gospel in Africa.[88] It is "a requirement for evangelization",[89] "a path towards full

[85] Cf. *ibid.* 6.
[86] JOHN PAUL II, Apostolic Exhortation *Catechesi Tradendae* (16 October 1979), 53: *AAS* 71 (1979), 1319.
[87] JOHN PAUL II, Encyclical Letter *Redemptoris Missio* (7 December 1990), 52: *AAS* 83 (1991), 229; cf. *Propositio* 28.
[88] Cf. *Propositio* 29.
[89] *Propositio* 30.

evangelization",[90] and one of the greatest challenges for the Church on the Continent on the eve of the Third Millennium.[91]

Theological foundations

60.   "But when the time had fully come" (Gal 4:4), the Word, the Second Person of the Blessed Trinity, the Only Son of God, "by the power of the Holy Spirit he became incarnate from the Virgin Mary, and was made man".[92] This is the sublime mystery of the Incarnation of the Word, a mystery which took place *in history:* in clearly defined circumstances of time and space, amidst a people with its own culture, a people that God had chosen and accompanied throughout the entire history of salvation, in order to show through what he did for them what he intended to do for the whole human race.

Jesus Christ is the unmistakable proof of God's love for humanity (cf. *Rom* 5:8). By his life, his preaching of the Good News to the poor, his Passion, Death and glorious Resurrection, he brought about the remission of our sins and our reconciliation with God, his Father and, thanks to him, our Father too. The Word that the Church proclaims is precisely the Word of God made man, who is himself the subject and object of this Word. *The Good News is Jesus Christ.*

---

[90]   *Propositio* 32.
[91]   Cf. *Propositio* 33.
[92]   Nicene-Constantinopolitan Creed: *DS* 150.

Just as "the Word became flesh and dwelt among us" (*Jn* 1:14), so too the Good News, the Word of Jesus Christ proclaimed to the nations, *must take root* in the life-situation of the hearers of the Word. Inculturation is precisely this insertion of the Gospel message into cultures.[93] For the Incarnation of the Son of God, precisely because it was complete and concrete,[94] was also an incarnation in a particular culture.

61.   Given the close and organic relationship that exists between Jesus Christ and the Word that the Church proclaims, the inculturation of the revealed message cannot but follow the "logic" proper to the *Mystery of the Redemption*. Indeed, the Incarnation of the Word is not an isolated moment but tends towards Jesus' "Hour" and the Paschal Mystery: "Unless a grain of wheat falls into the earth and dies, it remains alone; but if it dies, it bears much fruit" (*Jn* 12:24). Jesus says: "And I, when I am lifted up from the earth, will draw all men to myself" (*Jn* 12:32). This emptying of self, this *kenosis* necessary for exaltation, which is the way of Christ and of each of his disciples (cf. *Phil* 2:6-9), sheds light on the encounter of cultures with Christ and his *Gospel*. "Every culture needs to be transformed by Gospel values in the light of the Paschal Mystery".[95]

[93] Cf. JOHN PAUL II, Apostolic Exhortation *Catechesi Tradendae* (16 October 1979), 53: *AAS* 71 (1979), 1319.

[94] Cf. JOHN PAUL II, Address at the University of Coimbra, Coimbra (15 May 1982), 5: *Insegnamenti* V/2 (1982), 1695.

[95] *Propositio* 28.

It is by looking at the Mystery of the Incarnation and of the Redemption that the values and counter-values of cultures are to be discerned. Just as the Word of God became like us in everything but sin, so too the inculturation of the Good News takes on all authentic human values, purifying them from sin and restoring to them their full meaning.

Inculturation also has profound links with the *Mystery of Pentecost*. Thanks to the outpouring and action of the Spirit, who draws gifts and talents into unity, all the peoples of the earth when they enter the Church live a new Pentecost, profess in their own tongue the one faith in Jesus, and proclaim the marvels that the Lord has done for them. The Spirit, who on the natural level is the true source of the wisdom of peoples, leads the Church with a supernatural light into knowledge of the whole truth. In her turn the Church takes on the values of different cultures, becoming the *"sponsa ornata monilibus suis"*, "the bride who adorns herself with her jewels" (cf. *Is* 61:10).

Criteria and areas of inculturation

62.   Inculturation is a difficult and delicate task, since it raises the question of the Church's fidelity to the Gospel and the Apostolic Tradition amidst the constant evolution of cultures. Rightly therefore the Synod Fathers observed: "Considering the rapid changes in the cultural, social, economic and political domains, our local Churches must be involved in the process of inculturation in an ongoing manner, respecting the two following crite-

ria: compatibility with the Christian message and communion with the universal Church ... In all cases, care must be taken to avoid syncretism".[96]

"Inculturation is a movement towards full evangelization. It seeks to dispose people to receive Jesus Christ in an integral manner. It touches them on the personal, cultural, economic and political levels so that they can live a holy life in total union with God the Father, through the action of the Holy Spirit".[97]

Thanking God for the fruits which the efforts at inculturation have already brought forth in the life of the Churches of the Continent, notably in the ancient Eastern Churches of Africa, the Synod recommended "to the Bishops and to the Episcopal Conferences to take note that inculturation includes the whole life of the Church and the whole process of evangelization. It includes theology, liturgy, the Church's life and structures. All this underlines the need for research in the field of African cultures in all their complexity". Precisely for this reason the Synod invited Pastors "to exploit to the maximum the numerous possibilities which the Church's present discipline provides in this matter".[98]

The Church as God's Family

63.   Not only did the Synod speak of inculturation, but it also made use of it, taking the *Church*

---

[96] *Propositio* 31.
[97] *Propositio* 32.
[98] *Ibid.*

as *God's Family* as its guiding idea for the evangelization of Africa.[99] The Synod Fathers acknowledged it as an expression of the Church's nature particularly appropriate for Africa. For this image emphasizes care for others, solidarity, warmth in human relationships, acceptance, dialogue and trust.[100] The new evangelization will thus aim at *building up the Church as Family,* avoiding all ethnocentrism and excessive particularism, trying instead to encourage reconciliation and true communion between different ethnic groups, favouring solidarity and the sharing of personnel and resources among the particular Churches, without undue ethnic considerations.[101] "It is earnestly to be hoped that theologians in Africa will work out the theology of the Church as Family with all the riches contained in this concept, showing its complementarity with other images of the Church".[102]

All this presupposes a profound study of the heritage of Scripture and Tradition which the Second Vatican Council presented in the Dogmatic Constitution *Lumen Gentium.* This admirable text expounds the doctrine on the Church using images drawn from Sacred Scripture such as the Mystical Body, People of God, Temple of the Holy Spirit, Flock and Sheepfold, the House in which God dwells with man. According to the Council, the Church is the Bride of Christ, our

---

[99] Cf. SECOND VATICAN ECUMENICAL COUNCIL, Dogmatic Constitution on the Church *Lumen Gentium,* 6.
[100] Cf. *Propositio* 8.
[101] Cf. *ibid.*
[102] *Ibid.*

Mother, the Holy City and the first fruits of the coming Kingdom. These images will have to be taken into account when developing, according to the Synod's recommendation, an ecclesiology focused on the idea of the Church as the Family of God.[103] It will then be possible to appreciate in all its richness and depth the statement which is the Dogmatic Constitution's point of departure: "By her relationship with Christ, the Church is a kind of sacrament or sign of intimate union with God, and of the unity of all mankind".[104]

Areas of application

64.   In practice, and without any prejudice to the traditions proper to either the Latin or Eastern Church, "inculturation of the *liturgy,* provided it does not change the essential elements, should be carried out so that the faithful can better understand and live liturgical celebrations".[105]

The Synod also reaffirmed that, when doctrine is hard to assimilate even after a long period of evangelization, or when its practice poses serious pastoral problems, especially in the sacramental life, fidelity to the Church's teaching must be maintained. At the same time, people must be treated with justice and true pastoral charity. Bearing this in mind, the Synod expressed the hope that the Episcopal Conferences, in coopera-

---

[103] Cf. *ibid.*

[104] SECOND VATICAN ECUMENICAL COUNCIL, Dogmatic Constitution on the Church *Lumen Gentium,* 1. See also Chapters I and II.

[105] *Propositio* 34.

tion with Universities and Catholic Institutes, would set up study commissions, especially for matters concerning marriage, the veneration of ancestors, and the spirit world, in order to examine in depth all the cultural aspects of problems from the theological, sacramental, liturgical and canonical points of view.[106]

Dialogue

65. "Openness to dialogue is the Christian's attitude inside the community as well as with other believers and with men and women of good will".[107] *Dialogue is to be practised first of all within the family of the Church* at all levels: between Bishops, Episcopal Conferences or Hierarchical Assemblies and the Apostolic See, between Conferences or Episcopal Assemblies of the different nations of the same continent and those of other continents, and within each particular Church between the Bishop, the presbyterate, consecrated persons, pastoral workers and the lay faithful; and also between different rites within the same Church. SECAM is to establish "structures and means which will ensure the exercise of this dialogue",[108] especially in order to foster an organic pastoral solidarity.

"United to Jesus Christ by their witness in Africa, Catholics are invited to develop an *ecumenical dialogue* with all their baptized brothers

---

[106] Cf. *Propositiones* 35-37.
[107] *Propositio* 38.
[108] *Propositio* 39.

and sisters of other Christian denominations, in order that the unity for which Christ prayed may be achieved, and in order that their service to the peoples of the Continent may make the Gospel more credible in the eyes of those who are searching for God".[109] Such dialogue can be conducted through initiatives such as ecumenical translations of the Bible, theological study of various dimensions of the Christian faith or by bearing common evangelical witness to justice, peace and respect for human dignity. For this purpose care will be taken to set up national and diocesan commissions for ecumenism.[110] Together Christians are responsible for the witness to be borne to the Gospel on the Continent. Advances in ecumenism are also aimed at making this witness more effective.

66. "Commitment to dialogue must also embrace all Muslims of good will. Christians cannot forget that many Muslims try to imitate the faith of Abraham and to live the demands of the Decalogue".[111] In this regard the *Message of the Synod* emphasizes that the Living God, Creator of heaven and earth and the Lord of history, is the Father of the one great human family to which we all belong. As such, he wants us to bear witness to him through our respect for the values and religious traditions of each person, working together for human progress and development at all levels.

[109] *Propositio* 40.
[110] Cf. *ibid.*
[111] *Propositio* 41.

Far from wishing to be the one in whose name a person would kill other people, he requires believers to join together in the service of life in justice and peace.[112] Particular care will therefore be taken so that Islamic-Christian dialogue respects on both sides the principle of religious freedom with all that this involves, also including external and public manifestations of faith.[113] Christians and Muslims are called to commit themselves to promoting a dialogue free from the risks of false irenicism or militant fundamentalism, and to raising their voices against unfair policies and practices, as well as against the lack of reciprocity in matters of religious freedom.[114]

67.   With regard to African traditional religion, a serene and prudent dialogue will be able, on the one hand, to protect Catholics from negative influences which condition the way of life of many of them and, on the other hand, to foster the assimilation of positive values such as belief in a Supreme Being who is Eternal, Creator, Provident and Just Judge, values which are readily harmonized with the content of the faith. They can even be seen as a *preparation for the Gospel,* because they contain precious *semina Verbi* which can lead, as already happened in the past, a great number of people "to be open to the fullness of

---

[112] Cf. No. 23: *L'Osservatore Romano* (English-language edition), 11 May 1994, 7.
[113] Cf. *Propositio* 41.
[114] Cf. *ibid.*

Revelation in Jesus Christ through the proclamation of the Gospel".[115]

The adherents of African traditional religion should therefore be treated with great respect and esteem, and all inaccurate and disrespectful language should be avoided. For this purpose, suitable courses in African traditional religion should be given in houses of formation for priests and religious.[116]

Integral human development

68.   Integral human development — the development of every person and of the whole person, especially of the poorest and most neglected in the community — is at the very heart of evangelization. "Between evangelization and human advancement — development and liberation — there are in fact profound links. These include links of an anthropological order, because the man who is to be evangelized is not an abstract being but is subject to social and economic questions. They also include links in the theological order, since one cannot dissociate the plan of creation from the plan of Redemption. The latter plan touches the very concrete situations of injustice to be combatted and of justice to be restored. They include links of the eminently evangelical order, which is that of charity: how in fact can one proclaim the new commandment of love without

[115] *Propositio* 42.
[116] Cf. *ibid.*

promoting in justice and peace the true, authentic advancement of man?"[117]

When the Lord Jesus began his public ministry in the synagogue at Nazareth, he chose the Messianic text of the Book of the Prophet Isaiah in order to shed light on his mission: "The Spirit of the Lord God is upon me, because he has anointed me to preach good news to the poor. He has sent me to proclaim release to the captives and recovering of sight to the blind, to set at liberty those who are oppressed, to proclaim the acceptable year of the Lord" (*Lk* 4:18-19; cf. *Is* 61:1-2).

The Lord thus considers himself as sent to relieve human misery and combat every kind of neglect. He came to *liberate* humanity; he came to take upon himself our infirmities and diseases. "The entire ministry of Jesus is marked by the concern he showed to all those around him who were affected by suffering: persons in mourning, paralytics, lepers, the blind, the deaf, the mute (cf. *Mt* 8:17)".[118] "It is impossible to accept that in evangelization one could or should ignore the importance of the problems so much discussed today, concerning justice, liberation, development and peace in the world".[119] The liberation that evangelization proclaims "cannot be contained in the simple and restricted dimension of economics, poli-

---

[117] PAUL VI, Apostolic Exhortation *Evangelii Nuntiandi* (8 December 1975), 31: *AAS* 68 (1976), 26.

[118] SYNOD OF BISHOPS, Special Assembly for Africa, *Lineamenta*, 79.

[119] PAUL VI, Apostolic Exhortation *Evangelii Nuntiandi* (8 December 1975), 31: *AAS* 68 (1976), 26.

tics, social or cultural life; it must envisage the whole man, in all his aspects, right up to and including his openness to the absolute, even the Divine Absolute".[120]

The Second Vatican Council says so well: "Pursuing the saving purpose which is proper to her, the Church does not only communicate divine life to men but in some way casts the reflected light of that life over the entire earth, most of all by its healing and elevating impact on the dignity of the person, by the way in which it strengthens the seams of human society and imbues the everyday activity of men with a deeper meaning and importance. Thus through her individual members and her whole community, the Church believes she can contribute greatly towards making the family of man and its history more human".[121] The Church proclaims and begins to bring about the Kingdom of God after the example of Jesus, because "the Kingdom's nature ... is one of communion among all human beings — with one another and with God".[122] Thus "the Kingdom is the source of full liberation and total salvation for all people: with this in mind then, the Church walks and lives intimately *bound* in a real sense to their history".[123]

---

[120] *Ibid.*, 33: *loc. cit.*, 27.

[121] Pastoral Constitution on the Church in the Modern World *Gaudium et Spes*, 40.

[122] JOHN PAUL II, Encyclical Letter *Redemptoris Missio* (7 December 1990), 15: *AAS* 83 (1991), 263.

[123] JOHN PAUL II, Post-Synodal Apostolic Exhortation *Christifideles Laici* (30 December 1988), 36: *AAS* 81 (1989), 459.

69. Human history finds its true meaning in the Incarnation of the Word of God, who is the foundation of restored *human dignity*. It is through Christ, the "image of the invisible God, the first-born of all creation" (*Col* 1:15), that man is redeemed. "For by his Incarnation the Son of God has united himself in some fashion with every man".[124] How can we fail to exclaim with Saint Leo the Great: "Christian, recognize your dignity"?[125]

To proclaim Jesus Christ is therefore to *reveal to people their inalienable dignity,* received from God through the Incarnation of his Only Son. "Since it has been entrusted to the Church to reveal the mystery of God, who is the ultimate goal of man", continues the Second Vatican Council, "she opens up to man at the same time the meaning of his own existence, that is, the innermost truth about himself ".[126]

Endowed with this extraordinary dignity, people should not live in sub-human social, economic, cultural and political conditions. This is the theological foundation of the struggle for the defence of personal dignity, for justice and social peace, for the promotion, liberation and integral human development of all people and of every individual. It is also for this reason that the development of peoples — within each nation and among

---

[124] SECOND VATICAN ECUMENICAL COUNCIL, Pastoral Constitution on the Church in the Modern World *Gaudium et Spes*, 22.

[125] *Sermo* XXI, 3: *SCh* 22a, 72.

[126] Pastoral Constitution on the Church in the Modern World *Gaudium et Spes*, 41.

nations — must be achieved *in solidarity,* as my Predecessor Pope Paul VI so well observed.[127] Precisely for this reason he could affirm: "The new name for peace is development".[128] It can thus rightly be stated that "integral development implies respect for human dignity and this can only be achieved in justice and peace".[129]

Becoming the voice of the voiceless

70.   Strengthened by faith and hope in the saving power of Jesus, the Synod Fathers concluded their work by renewing their commitment to accept the challenge of being instruments of salvation in every area of the life of the peoples of Africa. "The Church", they declared, "must continue to exercise her prophetic role and be the voice of the voiceless",[130] so that everywhere the human dignity of every individual will be acknowledged, and that people will always be at the centre of all government programmes. The Synod "challenges the consciences of Heads of State and those responsible for the public domain to guarantee ever more the liberation and development of their peoples".[131] Only at this price is peace established between nations.

Evangelization must promote initiatives which contribute to the development and *ennoblement* of

---

[127] Cf. Encyclical Letter *Populorum Progressio* (26 March 1967), 48: *AAS* 59 (1967), 281.
[128] *Ibid.,* 87: *loc. cit.,* 299.
[129] *Propositio* 45.
[130] *Ibid.*
[131] *Ibid.*

individuals in their spiritual and material existence. This involves the development of every person and of the whole person, considered not only individually but also and especially in the context of the common and harmonious development of all the members of a nation and of all the peoples of the world.[132]

Finally, evangelization must denounce and combat all that degrades and destroys the person. "The condemnation of evils and injustices is also part of that *ministry of evangelization* in the social field which is an aspect of the Church's *prophetic role*. But it should be made clear that proclamation is always more important than condemnation, and the latter cannot ignore the former, which gives it true solidity and the force of higher motivation".[133]

Means of social communication

71.   "From the beginning it has been a characteristic of God to want to communicate. This he does by various means. He has bestowed being upon every created thing, animate or inanimate. He enters into relationships with human beings in a very special way. 'In many and various ways God spoke of old to our fathers by the prophets; but in these last days he as spoken to us by a Son'

---

[132] Cf. PAUL VI, Encyclical Letter *Populorum Progressio* (26 March 1967), 48: *AAS* 59 (1967), 281.

[133] JOHN PAUL II, Encyclical Letter *Sollicitudo Rei Socialis* (30 December 1987), 41: *AAS* 80 (1988), 572.

(*Heb* 1:1-2)".[134] The Word of God is by nature word, dialogue and communication. He came to restore on the one hand communication and relations between God and humanity, and on the other hand those of people with one another.

The Synod paid great attention to the mass media under two important and complementary aspects: as a new and emerging cultural world and as a series of means serving communication. First of all, they constitute a new culture that has its own language and above all its own specific values and counter-values. For this reason, like any culture, the mass media need to be evangelized.[135]

Today in fact the mass media constitute not only a world but also a culture and civilization. And it is also to this world that the Church is sent to bring the Good News of salvation. The heralds of the Gospel must therefore *enter this world* in order to *allow themselves to be permeated* by this new civilization and culture for the purpose of learning how to make good *use* of them. "The first Areopagus of the modern age is the world of communications, which is unifying humanity and turning it into what is known as a 'global village'. The means of social communication have become so important as to be for many the chief means of information and education, of guidance and inspira-

    [134] SYNOD OF BISHOPS, Special Assembly for Africa, *Instrumentum Laboris*, 127.
    [135] Cf. *Message of the Synod* (6 May 1994), 45-46: *L'Osservatore Romano* (English-language edition), 11 May 1994, 8.

tion in their behaviour as individuals, families and within society at large".[136]

Training in the use of the mass media is therefore a necessity not only *for the preacher* of the Gospel, who must master, among other things, the media *style* of communication but also for the *reader,* the *listener* and the *viewer.* Trained to understand this kind of communication, they must be able to make use of its contributions with discernment and a critical mind.

In Africa, where *oral transmission* is one of the characteristics of culture, such training is of capital importance. This same kind of communication must remind pastors, especially Bishops and priests, that the Church is sent to *speak,* to preach the Gospel in words and deeds. Thus she *cannot remain silent,* at the risk of failing in her mission, except in cases where silence itself would be a way of speaking and bearing witness. We must therefore always preach in season and out of season (cf. *2 Tim* 4:2), in order to build up, in charity and truth.

---

[136] JOHN PAUL II, Encyclical Letter *Redemptoris Missio* (7 December 1990), 37: *AAS* 83 (1991), 285.

CHAPTER IV

IN THE LIGHT OF THE THIRD CHRISTIAN MILLENNIUM

I. Present-Day Challenges

72. The Special Assembly for Africa of the Synod of Bishops was convoked so that the whole Church of God on the Continent might reflect on its evangelizing mission in the light of the Third Millennium and prepare, as I have said, "an organic pastoral solidarity within the entire African territory and nearby Islands".[137] Such a mission includes, as already mentioned, *urgent tasks and challenges, due to the profound and rapid changes in African societies* and to the effects of the emergence of a global civilization.

Need for Baptism

73. The first urgent task is of course evangelization itself. On the one hand, the Church must assimilate and live ever more fully the message which the Lord has entrusted to her. On the other hand, she must bear witness to this message and proclaim it to all who do not yet know Jesus Christ. It is indeed for them that the Lord said to

---

[137] Angelus (6 January 1989), 2: *Insegnamenti* XII/1 (1989), 40.

the Apostles: *"Go therefore and make disciples of all nations"* (*Mt* 28:19).

Just as at Pentecost, the goal of preaching the *kerygma* is to bring the hearer to *metanoia* and *Baptism:* "The proclamation of the word of God has *Christian conversion* as its aim: a complete and sincere adherence to Christ and his Gospel through faith".[138] Conversion to Christ moreover "is joined to Baptism not only because of the Church's practice, but also by the will of Christ himself, who sent the Apostles to make disciples of all nations and to baptize them (cf. *Mt* 28:19). Conversion is also joined to Baptism because of the intrinsic need to receive the fullness of new life in Christ. As Jesus says to Nicodemus: *'Truly, truly, I say to you, unless one is born of water and the Spirit, he cannot enter the Kingdom of God'* (*Jn* 3:5). In Baptism, in fact, we are born anew to the life of God's children, united to Jesus Christ and anointed in the Holy Spirit. Baptism is not simply a seal of conversion, a kind of *external sign* indicating conversion and attesting to it. Rather, it is a *Sacrament which signifies and effects* rebirth from the Spirit, establishes real and unbreakable bonds with the Blessed Trinity, and makes us members of the Body of Christ, which is the Church".[139] Therefore a journey of conversion that did not culminate in Baptism would stop half-way.

It is true that people of upright heart who, through no fault of their own have not been

---

[138] JOHN PAUL II, Encyclical Letter *Redemptoris Missio* (7 December 1990), 46: *AAS* 83 (1991), 292.

[139] *Ibid.*, 47: *loc. cit.*, 293-294.

reached by the proclamation of the Gospel but who live in harmony with their conscience according to God's law, will be saved by Christ and in Christ. For every human being there is always an *actual* call from God, which is waiting to be acknowledged and received (cf. 1 *Tim* 2:4). It is precisely in order to facilitate this recognition and acceptance that Christ's disciples are required not to rest until the Good News of salvation has been brought to all.

Urgency of evangelization

74.   The Name of Jesus Christ is the only one by which it has been decreed that we can be saved (cf. *Acts* 4:12). Because in Africa there are millions who are not yet evangelized, the Church is faced with the necessary and urgent task of *proclaiming the Good News to all, and leading those who hear it to Baptism and the Christian life.* "The urgency of missionary activity derives from the *radical newness of life* brought by Christ and lived by his followers. This new life is a gift from God, and people are asked to accept and develop it, if they wish to realize the fullness of their vocation in conformity to Christ".[140] This new life in the radical newness of the Gospel also involves certain breaks from the customs and culture of whatever people in the world, because the Gospel is never an internal product of a particular country but always comes "from outside", from on high. For

---

[140] *Ibid.*, 7: *loc. cit.*, 255-256.

the baptized the great challenge will always be that of leading a Christian life in conformity with the commitments of Baptism, the Sacrament which signifies death to sin and daily resurrection to new life (cf. *Rom* 6:4-5). Without this conformity, it will be difficult for Christ's disciples to be the *"salt of the earth"* and *"light of the world"* (*Mt* 5:13, 14). If the Church in Africa makes a vigorous and unhesitating commitment to this path, the Cross can be planted in every part of the Continent for the salvation of peoples not afraid to open their doors to the Redeemer.

Importance of formation

75.   In all areas of Church life formation is of primary importance. People who have never had the chance to learn cannot really know the truths of faith, nor can they perform actions which they have never been taught. For this reason "the whole community needs to be trained, motivated and empowered for evangelization, each according to his or her specific role within the Church".[141] This includes Bishops, priests, members of Institutes of Consecrated Life and Societies of Apostolic Life, members of Secular Institutes and all the lay faithful.

Missionary training has to have a special place. It is "the task of the local Church, assisted by missionaries and their Institutes, and by the

---

[141] SYNOD OF BISHOPS, Special Assembly for Africa, *Relatio ante disceptationem* (11 April 1994), 8: *L'Osservatore Romano*, 13 April 1994, 4.

personnel from the young Churches. This work must be seen not as peripheral but as central to the Christian life".[142]

The formation programme will especially include the training of the lay faithful, so that they will fully exercise their role of inspiring the temporal order — political, cultural, economic and social — with Christian principles, which is the specific task of the laity's vocation in the world. For this purpose competent and well motivated lay people need to be encouraged to enter politics.[143] By worthily carrying out the duties of public office they will be able to "advance the common good and prepare the way for the Gospel".[144]

Deepening the faith

76.   The Church in Africa, in order to evangelize, must begin "by being evangelized herself ... She needs to listen unceasingly to what she must believe, to her reasons for hoping, to the new commandment of love. She is the People of God immersed in the world, and often tempted by idols, and she always needs to hear the proclamation of the 'mighty works of God' ".[145]

[142] JOHN PAUL II, Encyclical Letter *Redemptoris Missio* (7 December 1990), 83: *AAS* 83 (1991), 329.

[143] Cf. SYNOD OF BISHOPS, Special Assembly for Africa, *Message of the Synod* (6 May 1994), 33: *L'Osservatore Romano* (English-language edition), 11 May 1994, 8.

[144] SECOND VATICAN ECUMENICAL COUNCIL, Decree on the Apostolate of the Laity *Apostolicam Actuositatem*, 14.

[145] PAUL VI, Apostolic Exhortation *Evangelii Nuntiandi* (8 December 1975), 15: *AAS* 68 (1976), 14.

In Africa today "formation in the faith ... too often stops at the elementary stage, and the sects easily profit from this ignorance".[146] A serious deepening of the faith is thus urgently needed, because the rapid evolution of society has given rise to new challenges linked to the phenomena notably of family uprooting, urbanization, unemployment, materialistic seductions of all kinds, a certain secularization and an intellectual upheaval caused by the avalanche of insufficiently critical ideas spread by the media.[147]

The power of witness

77.   Formation must aim to provide Christians not only with technical expertise in passing on more clearly the content of the faith but also with a profound personal conviction enabling them to bear effective witness to it in daily life. All those called to proclaim the Gospel will therefore seek to act with total docility to the Spirit, who "today, just as at the beginning of the Church, acts in every evangelizer who allows himself to be possessed and led by him".[148] "Techniques of evangelization are good, but even the most advanced ones could not replace the gentle action of the Spirit. Even the most thorough preparation of the evangelizer has no effect without the Holy Spirit.

[146] JOHN PAUL II, Address to the Episcopal Conference of Cameroon, Yaoundé (13 August 1985), 4: *Insegnamenti* VIII/2 (1985), 378.
[147] Cf. *ibid.*, 5: *loc. cit.*, 378.
[148] PAUL VI, Apostolic Exhortation *Evangelii Nuntiandi* (8 December 1975), 75: *AAS* 68 (1976), 65.

Without the Holy Spirit the most convincing dialectic has no power over the human heart. Without him the most highly developed schemes on a sociological or psychological basis are quickly seen to be quite valueless".[149]

Genuine witness by believers is essential to the authentic proclamation of the faith in Africa today. In particular they should show the witness of sincere mutual love. " 'This is eternal life, that they know you the only true God, and Jesus Christ whom you have sent' (*Jn* 17:3). The ultimate purpose of mission is to enable people to share in the communion which exists between the Father and the Son. The disciples are to live in unity with one another, remaining in the Father and the Son, so that the world may know and believe (cf. *Jn* 17:21-23). This is a very important missionary text. It makes us understand that we are missionaries above all because of *what we are,* a Church whose innermost life is unity in love, even before we become missionaries *in word and deed*".[150]

Inculturating the faith

78.   By reason of its deep conviction that *"the synthesis between culture and faith is not only a demand of culture but also of faith"*, because "a faith that does not become culture is not fully accepted,

---

[149] *Ibid.: loc. cit.*, 65-66.
[150] JOHN PAUL II, Encyclical Letter *Redemptoris Missio* (7 December 1990), 23: *AAS* 83 (1991), 269-270.

not entirely thought out, not faithfully lived", [151] the Special Assembly for Africa of the Synod of Bishops considered inculturation a priority and an urgent task in the life of Africa's particular Churches. Only in this way can the Gospel be firmly implanted in the Continent's Christian communities. Following in the footsteps of the Second Vatican Council, [152] the Synod Fathers interpreted inculturation as a process that includes the whole of Christian existence — theology, liturgy, customs, structures — without of course compromising what is of divine right and the great discipline of the Church, confirmed in the course of centuries by remarkable fruits of virtue and heroism. [153]

The challenge of inculturation in Africa consists in ensuring that the followers of Christ will ever more fully assimilate the Gospel message, while remaining faithful to all authentic African values. Inculturation of the faith in every area of Christian and human life is an arduous task which can only be carried out with the help of the Spirit of the Lord who leads the Church to the whole truth (cf. *Jn* 16:13).

[151] JOHN PAUL II, Address to the Italian National Congress of the Ecclesial Movement for Cultural Commitment (16 January 1982), 2: *Insegnamenti* V/1 (1982), 131.

[152] Cf. Decree on the Missionary Activity of the Church *Ad Gentes*, 22.

[153] Cf. *Propositio* 32; SECOND VATICAN ECUMENICAL COUNCIL, Constitution on the Sacred Liturgy *Sacrosanctum Concilium*, 37-40.

A reconciled community

79.   The challenge of dialogue is fundamentally the challenge of transforming relationships between individuals, nations and peoples in religious, political, economic, social and cultural life. It is the challenge of Christ's love for all people, a love that the disciple must reproduce in his own life: "By this all men will know that you are my disciples, if you have love for one another" (*Jn* 13:35).

"Evangelization continues the dialogue of God with humanity and reaches its apex in the person of Jesus Christ".[154] Through the Cross he brought an end in himself to the hostility which divides people and keeps them apart (cf. *Eph* 2:16).

Despite the modern civilization of the "global village", in Africa as elsewhere in the world the spirit of dialogue, peace and reconciliation is far from dwelling in the hearts of everyone. Wars, conflicts and racist and xenophobic attitudes still play too large a role in the world of human relations.

The Church in Africa is aware that it has to become for all, through the witness borne by its own sons and daughters, a place of true reconciliation. Forgiven and mutually reconciled, these sons and daughters will thus be able to bring to the world the forgiveness and reconciliation which Christ our Peace (cf. *Eph* 2:14) offers to humanity

---

[154] *Propositio* 38.

through his Church. Otherwise the world will look more and more like a battlefield, where only selfish interests count and the *law of force* prevails, the law which fatally distances humanity from the hoped-for *civilization of love.*

II. THE FAMILY

Evangelizing the family

80.   "The future of the world and of the Church passes through the family".[155] Not only is the Christian family the first cell of the living ecclesial community, it is also the fundamental cell of society. In Africa in particular, the family is the foundation on which the social edifice is built. This is why the Synod considered the evangelization of the African family a major priority, if the family is to assume in its turn the role of *active subject* in view of the evangelization of families through families.

From the pastoral point of view, this is a real challenge, given the political, economic, social and cultural difficulties which African families must face as a result of the great changes which characterize contemporary society. While adopting the positive values of modernity, the African family must preserve its own essential values.

---

[155] JOHN PAUL II, Apostolic Exhortation *Familiaris Consortio* (22 November 1981), 75: *AAS* 74 (1982), 173.

The Holy Family as a model

81.   In this regard the Holy Family, which according to the Gospel (cf. *Mt* 2:14-15) lived for a time in Africa, is the *"prototype and example for all Christian families"* [156] and the *model and spiritual source* for every Christian family. [157]

To repeat the words of Pope Paul VI, pilgrim to the Holy Land: "The home of Nazareth is the school where we begin to understand the life of Jesus — the school of the *Gospel* ... Here, in this school, one learns why it is necessary to have a spiritual rule of life, if one wishes to follow the teaching of the Gospel and become a disciple of Christ". [158] In his profound meditation on the mystery of Nazareth, Pope Paul VI invites us to learn a threefold lesson: of *silence,* of *family life* and of *work.* In the home of Nazareth each one lives his or her own mission in perfect harmony with the other members of the Holy Family.

Dignity and role of man and woman

82.   The dignity of man and woman derives from the fact that when God created man, *"in the image of God* he created him, male and female he created them" (*Gen* 1:27). Both man and woman are created "in the image of God", that is, endowed with intelligence and will and therefore

---

[156] *Ibid.*, 86: *loc. cit.*, 189-190.
[157] Cf. *Propositio* 14.
[158] Homily in the Basilica of the Annunciation, Nazareth (5 January 1964): *AAS* 56 (1964), 167.

with freedom. The account of our first parents' sin confirms this (cf. *Gen 3*). The Psalmist sings of man's incomparable dignity: "Yet you have made him little less than a god; with glory and honour you crowned him, gave him power over the works of your hand, put all things under his feet" (*Ps* 8:6-7).

Having both been created in the image of God, man and woman, although different, are *essentially equal* from the point of view of their humanity. "From the very beginning, both are persons, unlike the other living beings in the world about them. The woman is another 'I' in a common humanity",[159] and each is a help for the other (cf. *Gen* 2:18-25).

"In creating the human race 'male and female', God gives man and woman an equal personal dignity, endowing them with inalienable rights and responsibilities proper to the human person".[160] The Synod deplored those African customs and practices "which deprive women of their rights and the respect due to them"[161] and asked the Church on the Continent to make every effort to foster the safeguarding of these rights.

[159] JOHN PAUL II, Apostolic Letter *Mulieris Dignitatem*, (15 August 1988), 6: *AAS* 80 (1988), 1662-1664; cf. *Letter to Women* (29 June 1995), 7: *L'Osservatore Romano* (English-language edition), 12 July 1995, 2.
   [160] JOHN PAUL II, Apostolic Exhortation *Familiaris Consortio* (22 November 1981), 22: *AAS* 74 (1982), 107.
   [161] *Propositio* 48.

83. God — Father, Son and Holy Spirit — is love (cf. *1 Jn* 4:8). "The communion between God and his people finds its definitive fulfilment in Jesus Christ, the Bridegroom who loves and gives himself as the Saviour of humanity, uniting it to himself as his Body. He reveals the original truth of marriage, the truth of the 'beginning', and, freeing man from his hardness of heart, he makes man capable of realizing this truth in its entirety. This revelation reaches its definitive fullness in the gift of love which the Word of God makes to humanity in assuming a human nature, and in the sacrifice which Jesus Christ makes of himself on the Cross for his Bride, the Church. In this sacrifice there is entirely revealed that plan which God has imprinted on the humanity of man and woman since their creation (cf. *Eph* 5:32-33); the Marriage of baptized persons thus becomes a *real symbol of that new and eternal Covenant* sanctioned in the Blood of Christ".[162]

The mutual love of baptized spouses makes present the love of Christ for his Church. As a sign of this love of Christ, Marriage is a *Sacrament of the New Covenant*: "Spouses are therefore the *permanent reminder* to the Church of what happened on the Cross; they are for one another and for the children *witnesses* to the salvation in which the Sacrament makes them sharers. Of this salva-

---

[162] JOHN PAUL II, Apostolic Exhortation *Familiaris Consortio* (22 November 1981), 13: *AAS* 74 (1982), 93-94.

tion event Marriage, like every sacrament, is a memorial, actuation and prophecy".[163]

Marriage is therefore a state of life, a way of Christian holiness, a vocation which is meant to lead to the glorious resurrection and to the Kingdom, where "they neither marry nor are given in marriage" (*Mt* 22:30). Marriage thus demands an indissoluble love; thanks to this stability it can contribute effectively to the complete fulfilment of the spouses' baptismal vocation.

Saving the African family

84.   Many interventions in the Synod Hall highlighted present-day threats to the African family. The concerns of the Synod Fathers were all the more justified in that the preparatory document of a United Nations Conference held in September 1994 in Cairo — on African soil — clearly seemed to wish to adopt resolutions contradicting many values of the African family. The Synod Fathers, accepting my concerns previously expressed to the Conference and to all the world's Heads of State,[164] launched an urgent appeal to safeguard the family. They pleaded: "Do not allow the African family to be ridiculed on its own soil! Do not allow the International Year of the Family to become the year of the destruction of the family!"[165]

[163] *Ibid.*
[164] Cf. Message to Mrs Nafis Sadik, Secretary General of the 1994 International Conference on Population and Development (18 March 1994): *AAS* 87 (1995), 190-196.
[165] *Message of the Synod* (6 May 1994), 30: *L'Osservatore Romano* (English-language edition), 11 May 1994, 7.

The family as open to society

85.   By its nature marriage, which has the special mission of perpetuating humanity, transcends the couple. In the same way, by its nature, the family extends beyond the individual household: it is oriented towards society. "The family has vital and organic links with society, since it is its foundation and nourishes it continually through its role of service to life: it is from the family that citizens come to birth and it is within the family that they find the first school of the social virtues that are the animating principle of the existence and development of society itself. Thus, far from being closed in on itself, the family is by nature and vocation open to other families and to society, and undertakes its social role".[166]

Along these lines, the Special Assembly for Africa affirmed that the goal of evangelization is to build up the Church as the Family of God, an anticipation on earth, though imperfect, of the Kingdom. The Christian families of Africa will thus become true "domestic churches", contributing to society's progress towards a more fraternal life. This is how African societies will be transformed through the Gospel!

---

[166] John Paul II, Apostolic Exhortation *Familiaris Consortio* (22 November 1981), 42: *AAS* 74 (1982), 134.

CHAPTER V

"YOU SHALL BE MY WITNESSES" IN AFRICA

Witness and holiness

86.   The challenges mentioned show how opportune the Special Assembly for Africa of the Synod of Bishops was: the Church's task in Africa is immense; in order to face it everyone's cooperation is necessary. *Witness* is an essential element of this cooperation. Christ challenges his disciples in Africa and gives them the mandate which he gave to the Apostles on the day of his Ascension: "You shall be my witnesses" (*Acts* 1:8) in Africa.

87.   The proclamation of the Good News by word and deed opens people's hearts to the desire for *holiness*, for being configured to Christ. In his First Letter to the Corinthians, Saint Paul addresses "those sanctified in Christ Jesus, called to be saints, together with all those who in every place call on the name of our Lord Jesus Christ" (1:2). Preaching the Gospel also aims to build up the Church of God, in the light of the coming of the Kingdom, which Christ will hand over to the Father at the end of time (cf. *1 Cor* 15:24).

"Entrance into the Kingdom of God demands a change of mentality (*metanoia*) and behaviour and a life of witness in word and deed, a life nourished in the Church by the reception of the sacra-

93

ments, particularly the Eucharist, the Sacrament of salvation".[167]

Inculturation, through which the faith penetrates the life of individuals and their primary communities, is also a path to holiness. Just as in the Incarnation Christ assumed human nature in everything but sin, analogously through inculturation the Christian message assimilates the values of the society to which it is proclaimed, rejecting whatever is marked by sin. To the extent that an ecclesial community can integrate the positive values of a specific culture, inculturation becomes an instrument by which the community opens itself to the riches of Christian holiness. An inculturation wisely carried out purifies and elevates the cultures of the various peoples.

From this point of view the *liturgy* is called to play an important role. As an effective way of proclaiming and living the mysteries of salvation, the liturgy can make a valid contribution towards the elevation and enrichment of specific manifestations of the culture of a people. It will therefore be the task of competent authority to see to the inculturation of those liturgical elements which, following artistically worthy models, can be changed in the light of current norms.[168]

I. AGENTS OF EVANGELIZATION

88.   Evangelization needs agents. For "how are men to call upon him [the Lord] in whom they

---

[167] *Propositio 5.*
[168] Cf. *Propositio 34.*

have not believed? And how are they to believe in him of whom they have never heard? And how are they to hear without a preacher? And how can men preach unless they are sent?" (*Rom* 10:14-15). The proclamation of the Gospel can be fully carried out only through the contribution of all believers at every level of the universal and local Church.

It is especially the concern of the local Church, entrusted to the responsibility of the Bishop, to coordinate the commitment to evangelization by gathering the faithful together, confirming them in the faith through the work of the priests and catechists, and supporting them in the fulfilment of their respective tasks. In order to accomplish this, the Diocese is to establish the necessary structures for getting together, dialogue and planning. By making use of these structures the Bishop will be able to guide in a suitable manner the work of priests, religious and laity, welcoming the gifts and charisms of each one, in order to put them at the service of an updated and clearsighted plan of pastoral action. The different Councils provided for by the current norms of Canon Law are to be considered a great help in contributing to this end.

Vital Christian communities

89. Right from the beginning, the Synod Fathers recognized that the Church as Family cannot reach her full potential as Church unless she is divided into communities small enough to foster

close human relationships. The Assembly described the characteristics of such communities as follows: primarily they should be places engaged in evangelizing themselves, so that subsequently they can bring the Good News to others; they should moreover be communities which pray and listen to God's Word, encourage the members themselves to take on responsibility, learn to live an ecclesial life, and reflect on different human problems in the light of the Gospel. Above all, these communities are to be committed to living Christ's love for everybody, a love which transcends the limits of the natural solidarity of clans, tribes or other interest groups.[169]

Laity

90. The laity are to be helped to become increasingly aware of their role in the Church, thereby fulfilling their particular mission as baptized and confirmed persons, according to the teaching of the Post-Synodal Apostolic Exhortation *Christifideles Laici* [170] and the Encyclical Letter *Redemptoris Missio*.[171] Lay people are to be trained for their mission through suitable centres and schools of biblical and pastoral formation. Similarly, Christians who occupy positions of responsibility are to be carefully prepared for political,

---

[169] Cf. *Propositio* 9.
[170] Cf. JOHN PAUL II, Post-Synodal Apostolic Exhortation *Christifideles Laici* (30 December 1988), 45-56: *AAS* 81 (1989), 481-506.
[171] Cf. JOHN PAUL II, Encyclical Letter *Redemptoris Missio* (7 December 1990), 71-74: *AAS* 83 (1991), 318-322.

economic and social tasks by means of a solid formation in the Church's social doctrine, so that in their places of work they will be faithful witnesses to the Gospel.[172]

Catechists

91.   "The role of the catechist has been and remains a determinative force in the implantation and expansion of the Church in Africa. The Synod recommends that catechists not only receive a sound initial formation ... but that they continue to receive doctrinal formation as well as moral and spiritual support".[173] Both Bishops and priests are to have their catechists at heart, seeing to it that they are guaranteed suitable living and working conditions so that they carry out their mission properly. In the midst of the Christian community the catechists' responsibility is to be acknowledged and held in respect.

The family

92.   The Synod launched an explicit appeal for each African Christian family to become "a privileged place for evangelical witness",[174] a true "domestic church",[175] a community which believes

---

[172] Cf. *Propositio* 12.
[173] *Propositio* 13.
[174] *Propositio* 14.
[175] SECOND VATICAN ECUMENICAL COUNCIL, Dogmatic Constitution on the Church *Lumen Gentium*, 11.

and evangelizes,[176] a community in dialogue with God [177] and generously open to the service of humanity.[178] "It is in the heart of the family that parents are by word and example ... the first heralds of the faith with regard to their children".[179] "It is here that the father of the family, the mother, children, and all members of the family exercise the *priesthood of the baptized* in a privileged way 'by the reception of the sacraments, prayer and thanksgiving, the witness of a holy life and self-denial and active charity'. Thus the home is the first school of Christian life and 'a school for human enrichment' ".[180]

Parents are to see to the Christian education of their children. With the practical help offered by strong, serene and committed Christian families, Dioceses will develop a programme for the family apostolate as part of their overall pastoral plan. The Christian family, as a "domestic Church" built on the solid cultural pillars and noble values of the African tradition of the family, is called upon to be a powerful nucleus of Christian witness in a society undergoing rapid and profound changes. The Synod felt this challenge

---

[176] Cf. JOHN PAUL II, Apostolic Exhortation *Familiaris Consortio* (22 November 1981), 52: *AAS* 74 (1982), 144-145.

[177] Cf. *ibid.*, 55: *loc. cit.*, 147-148.

[178] Cf. *ibid.*, 62: *loc. cit.*, 155.

[179] *Catechism of the Catholic Church*, No. 1656, which quotes the SECOND VATICAN ECUMENICAL COUNCIL, Dogmatic Constitution on the Church *Lumen Gentium*, 11.

[180] *Catechism of the Catholic Church*, No. 1657, which quotes the SECOND VATICAN ECUMENICAL COUNCIL, Dogmatic Constitution on the Church *Lumen Gentium*, 10; and the Pastoral Constitution on the Church in the Modern World *Gaudium et Spes*, 52.

with a particular urgency because the Church was then celebrating the Year of the Family with the rest of the international community.

Young people

93.   The Church in Africa knows well that youth are not only the present but above all the future of humanity. It is thus necessary to help young people to overcome the obstacles thwarting their development: illiteracy, idleness, hunger, drugs.[181] In order to meet these challenges, young people themselves should be called upon to become the evangelizers of their peers. No one can do this better than they. The *pastoral care of youth* must clearly be a part of the overall pastoral plan of Dioceses and parishes, so that young people will be enabled to discover very early on the value of the gift of self, an essential means for the person to reach maturity.[182] In this regard, the celebration of World Youth Day is a privileged instrument for the pastoral care of youth, which favours their formation through prayer, study and reflection.

Consecrated men and women

94.   "In the Church understood as the Family of God, *consecrated life* has the particular function not only of indicating to all the call to holiness but also of witnessing to fraternal life in community.

---

[181] Cf. *Propositio* 15.
[182] Cf. *ibid.*

99

Therefore, all who live the consecrated life are called to respond to their vocation in a spirit of communion and cooperation with the respective Bishops, clergy and laity".[183]

In the present-day circumstances of the mission in Africa, it is necessary to foster religious vocations to the contemplative and active life, above all choosing them with great discernment, and then seeing that they receive an integral human formation, as well as one which is solid in its spiritual and doctrinal, apostolic and missionary, biblical and theological dimensions. This formation is to be faithfully and regularly updated down through the years. With regard to the foundation of new Religious Institutes, great prudence and enlightened discernment are needed, and the criteria laid down by the Second Vatican Council and the canonical norms now in force are to be followed.[184] Once established, these Institutes are to be helped in acquiring juridical status and becoming autonomous in the management both of their own works and of their respective sources of income.

The Synodal Assembly, having stated that "Religious Institutes that do not have houses in Africa" are not authorized "to come seeking new vocations without prior dialogue with the local

---

[183] *Propositio* 16, which refers to the SECOND VATICAN ECUMENICAL COUNCIL, Dogmatic Constitution on the Church *Lumen Gentium*, 43-47.
[184] Cf. SECOND VATICAN ECUMENICAL COUNCIL, Decree on the Missionary Activity of the Church *Ad Gentes*, 18; and Decree on the Appropriate Renewal of the Religious Life *Perfectae Caritatis*, 19.

Ordinary",[185] then urged the leaders of the local Churches and of the Institutes of Consecrated Life and the Societies of Apostolic Life to foster dialogue among themselves, in order to create, in the spirit of the Church as Family, mixed groups for consultation which would serve as a witness to fraternity and as a sign of unity in the service of a common mission.[186] In this light, I have also accepted the request of the Synod Fathers to revise, if necessary, some points in the document *Mutuae Relationes*,[187] in order to define better the role of religious life in the local Church.[188]

Future priests

95.   The Synod Fathers affirmed that "today more than ever there is need to form *future priests* in the true cultural values of their country, in a sense of honesty, responsibility and integrity. They shall be formed in such a manner that they will have the qualities of the representatives of Christ, of true servants and animators of the Christian community ... solidly spiritual, ready to serve, dedicated to evangelization, capable of administering the goods of the Church efficiently and openly, and of living a simple life as befits their milieu".[189]

---

[185] *Propositio* 16.
[186] Cf. *Propositio* 22.
[187] CONGREGATION FOR RELIGIOUS AND SECULAR INSTITUTES and CONGREGATION FOR BISHOPS, Directives for Mutual Relations between Bishops and Religious in the Church *Mutuae Relationes* (14 May 1978): *AAS* 70 (1978), 473-506.
[188] Cf. *Propositio* 22.
[189] *Propositio* 18.

While respecting the traditions proper to the Eastern Churches, seminarians "should acquire affective maturity and should be both clear in their minds and deeply convinced that for the priest celibacy is inseparable from chastity".[190] Moreover "they should receive adequate formation on the meaning and place of consecration to Christ in the priesthood".[191]

Deacons

96.   Where pastoral conditions lend themselves to respect and understanding of this ancient ministry in the Church, Episcopal Conferences and Assemblies are to study the most suitable ways of promoting and encouraging the permanent diaconate "as an ordained ministry and also as an instrument of evangelization".[192] Where deacons already exist they should be provided with an integrated and thorough programme of permanent formation.

Priests

97.   Deeply grateful to all the priests — diocesan and members of Institutes — for the apostolic work they are doing and aware of the demands made by the evangelization of the peoples of Africa and Madagascar, the Synodal Assembly urged priests to live their "faithfulness to their vocation in the total gift of self to their

[190] Ibid.
[191] Ibid.
[192] Propositio 17.

mission and in full communion with their Bishop".[193] As for the Bishops, they are to see to the ongoing formation of priests, especially in the first years of their ministry,[194] helping them especially to deepen their understanding of sacred celibacy and to persevere in living it faithfully, recognizing "this surpassing gift which the Father has given them, and which the Lord praised so openly. Let them keep in mind the great mysteries which are signified and fulfilled in it."[195] This formation programme is also to give particular attention to the wholesome values present in the priests' surroundings. It is appropriate moreover to mention that the Second Vatican Council encouraged among priests "a certain common life", that is some kind of community life in the different forms suggested by real personal and pastoral needs. This will contribute towards the growth of the spiritual and intellectual life, of apostolic and pastoral ministry, of charity and mutual support, especially with regard to priests who are elderly, sick or in difficulty.[196]

Bishops

98.   The Bishops themselves will carefully pastor the Church which God obtained with the

[193] *Propositio* 20.

[194] Cf. JOHN PAUL II, Post-Synodal Apostolic Exhortation *Pastores Dabo Vobis* (25 March 1992), 70-77: *AAS* 84 (1992), 778-796; *Propositio* 20.

[195] SECOND VATICAN ECUMENICAL COUNCIL, Decree on the Ministry and Life of Priests *Presbyterorum Ordinis*, 16.

[196] Cf. *ibid.,* 8.

Blood of his own Son, fulfilling the responsibility entrusted to them by the Holy Spirit (cf. *Acts* 20:28). According to the recommendation of the Second Vatican Council, Bishops dedicated to carrying out "their Apostolic office as witnesses of Christ before all people" [197] are to exercise personally, in a spirit of trusting cooperation with the presbyterate and other pastoral workers, an irreplaceable service of unity in charity, carefully fulfilling their responsibilities of teaching, sanctifying and governing. Moreover they are regularly to update themselves theologically and to foster their spiritual life, taking part as much as possible in the sessions of renewal and formation organized by the Episcopal Conferences or the Apostolic See.[198] In particular, they should never forget the admonition of Pope Saint Gregory the Great, according to whom the Pastor is the light of his faithful above all through an exemplary moral conduct marked by holiness.[199]

II. STRUCTURES OF EVANGELIZATION

99.   It is a source of joy and comfort to note that "the laity are more and more engaged in the mission of the Church in Africa and Madagascar", thanks especially "to the dynamism of Catholic

---

[197] Decree on the Bishops' Pastoral Office in the Church *Christus Dominus*, 11.

[198] Cf. *Propositio* 21.

[199] Cf. *Epistolarum Liber*, VIII, 33: PL 77, 935.

Action movements, apostolic associations and new spiritual movements".[200] The Synod Fathers requested that this thrust be pursued and developed among all the laity: adults, youth and children.

Parishes

100. By its nature the parish is the ordinary place where the faithful worship and live their Christian life. In it they can express and practise the initiatives which faith and Christian charity bring to the attention of the community of believers. The parish is the place which manifests the *communion of various groups and movements*, which find in it spiritual sustenance and material support. Priests and lay people will see to it that parish life is harmonious, expressing the Church as Family, where all devote "themselves to the Apostles' teaching and fellowship, to the breaking of bread and the prayers" (*Acts* 2:42).

Movements and associations

101. A fraternal harmony which bears living witness to the Gospel will also be the goal of apostolic movements and religious associations. In them the lay faithful truly find a privileged opportunity to be the "leaven in the dough" (cf. *Mt* 13:33), especially in areas concerned with the administration of temporal goods according to

---

[200] *Propositio* 23; cf. *Relatio ante disceptationem* (11 April 1994), 11: *L'Osservatore Romano*, 13 April 1994, 4.

God's plan and the struggle for the promotion of human dignity, justice and peace.

Schools

102.   "Catholic schools are at one and the same time places of evangelization, well-rounded education, inculturation and initiation to the dialogue of life among young people of different religions and social backgrounds".[201] The Church in Africa and Madagascar should therefore make its own contribution to the fostering of "education for all" [202] in Catholic schools, without neglecting "the Christian education of pupils in non-Catholic schools. For university students there will be a programme of religious formation which corresponds to the level of studies".[203] These contributions presuppose the human, cultural and religious formation of the educators themselves.

Universities and Higher Institutes

103.   "The Catholic Universities and Higher Institutes in Africa have a prominent role to play in the proclamation of the salvific Word of God. They are a sign of the growth of the Church insofar as their research integrates the truths and experiences of the faith and helps to internalize them. They serve the Church by providing trained personnel, by studying important theological and

---

[201] *Propositio* 24.
[202] *Ibid.*
[203] *Ibid.*

social questions for the benefit of the Church, by developing an African theology, by promoting the work of inculturation especially in liturgical celebration, by publishing books and publicizing Catholic truth, by undertaking assignments given by the Bishops and by contributing to a scientific study of cultures".[204]

In this time of generalized social upheaval on the Continent, the Christian faith can shed helpful light on African society. *"Catholic cultural centres offer to the Church the possibility of presence and action in the field of cultural change. They constitute in effect public forums which allow the Church to make widely known, in creative dialogue, Christian convictions about man, woman, family, work, economy, society, politics, international life, the environment"*.[205] Thus they are places of listening, respect and tolerance.

Material means

104. Precisely in this context the Synod Fathers emphasized how necessary it is for each Christian community to be organized so that as far as possible it can provide for its own needs.[206] Besides qualified personnel, evangelization requires material and financial means, and Dioceses are often far from possessing them in sufficient measure. It is therefore urgent that the particular

---

[204] *Propositio* 25.
[205] *Propositio* 26.
[206] Cf. SECOND VATICAN ECUMENICAL COUNCIL, Decree on the Missionary Activity of the Church *Ad Gentes*, 15.

Churches in Africa have the objective of providing for their own needs as soon as possible, thereby assuring their self-sufficiency. Consequently, I earnestly invite the Episcopal Conferences, Dioceses and all the Christian communities of the Continent's Churches, insofar as it is within their competence, to see to it that this self-sufficiency becomes increasingly evident. At the same time, I call on sister Churches all over the world to be more generous to the Pontifical Mission Aid Societies so that, through their structures of assistance, they will be able to offer to poorer Dioceses economic assistance dedicated to projects that will generate resources, with a view to increasing the financial self-reliance of the Churches.[207] Lastly, we cannot forget that a Church is able to reach material and financial independence only if the people entrusted to it do not live in conditions of extreme poverty.

---

[207] Cf. *Propositio* 27.

CHAPTER VI

BUILDING THE KINGDOM OF GOD

Kingdom of justice and peace

105.   The mandate that Jesus gave to his disciples at the moment of his Ascension into heaven is addressed to the Church of God in all times and places. The Church as the Family of God in Africa must bear witness to Christ also by promoting justice and peace on the Continent and throughout the world. The Lord says: "Blessed are the peacemakers, for they shall be called sons of God. Blessed are those who are persecuted for righteousness' sake, for theirs is the Kingdom of heaven" (*Mt* 5:9-10). The Church's witness must be accompanied by a firm commitment to justice and solidarity by each member of God's People. This is especially important for the lay faithful who hold public office, because such witness demands an abiding spiritual attitude and a way of life consistent with the Christian faith.

Ecclesial dimension of witness

106.   The Synod Fathers drew attention to the ecclesial dimension of this witness and solemnly

declared: "The Church must continue to play her prophetic role and be the voice of the voiceless".[208]

But to achieve this effectively, the Church, as a community of faith, must be an energetic witness to justice and peace in her structures and in the relationships among her members. The *Message of the Synod* courageously states: "The Churches in Africa are also aware that, insofar as their own internal affairs are concerned, justice is not always respected with regard to those men and women who are at their service. If the Church is to give witness to justice, she recognizes that whoever dares to speak to others about justice should also strive to be just in their eyes. It is necessary therefore to examine with care the procedures, the possessions and the life style of the Church".[209]

In what concerns the promotion of justice and especially the defence of fundamental human rights, the Church's apostolate cannot be improvised. Aware that in many African countries gross violations of human dignity and rights are being perpetrated, I ask the Episcopal Conferences to establish, where they do not yet exist, Justice and Peace Commissions at various levels. These will awaken Christian communities to their evangelical responsibilities in the defence of human rights.[210]

---

[208] *Propositio* 45.

[209] No. 43: *L'Osservatore Romano* (English-language edition), 11 May 1994, 8.

[210] Cf. *Propositio* 46.

107.   If the proclamation of justice and peace is an integral part of the task of evangelization, it follows that the promotion of these values should also be a part of the pastoral programme of each Christian community. That is why I urge that all pastoral agents are to be adequately trained for this apostolate. "The formation of clergy, religious and laity, imparted in the areas of their apostolate, should lay emphasis on the social teaching of the Church. Each person, according to his state of life, should be specially trained to know his rights and duties, the meaning and service of the common good, honest management of public goods and the proper manner of participating in political life, in order to be able to act in a credible manner in the face of social injustices".[211]

As a body organized within the community and the nation, the Church has both the right and the duty to participate fully in building a just and peaceful society with all the means at her disposal. Here we must mention the Church's apostolate in the areas of education, health care, social awareness and in other programmes of assistance. In the measure that these activities help to reduce ignorance, improve public health and promote a greater participation of all in solving the problems of society in a spirit of freedom and co-responsibility, the Church creates conditions for the progress of justice and peace.

---

[211] *Propositio* 47.

108.   In the pluralistic societies of our day, it is especially due to the commitment of Catholics in public life that the Church can exercise a positive influence. Whether they be professionals or teachers, businessmen or civil servants, law enforcement agents or politicians, Catholics are expected to bear witness to goodness, truth, justice and love of God in their daily life. "The task of the faithful lay person ... is to be the salt of the earth and light of the world, especially in those places where only a lay person is able to render the Church present".[212]

Cooperation with other believers

109.   The obligation to commit oneself to the development of peoples is not just an *individual* duty, and still less an *individualistic* one, as if it were possible to achieve this development through the isolated efforts of each person. It is a responsibility which obliges *each and every man and woman*, as well as *societies and nations*. In particular, it obliges the Catholic Church and the other Churches and Ecclesial Communities, with which Catholics are willing to cooperate in this field.[213] In this sense, just as Catholics invite their Christian

---

[212] SYNOD OF BISHOPS, Special Assembly for Africa, *Message of the Synod* (6 May 1994), 57: *L'Osservatore Romano* (English-language edition), 11 May 1994, 9.

[213] Cf. JOHN PAUL II, Encyclical Letter *Ut Unum Sint* (25 May 1995), 40: *L'Osservatore Romano* (English-language edition), 31 May 1995, Supplement, VI.

brothers and sisters to share in their initiatives, so, when they accept invitations offered to them, Catholics show that they are ready to cooperate in projects undertaken by other Christians. In the promotion of integral human development Catholics can also cooperate with the believers of other religions, as in fact they are already doing in various places.[214]

Good administration of public affairs

110.   The Synod Fathers were unanimous in acknowledging that the greatest challenge for bringing about justice and peace in Africa consists in a good administration of public affairs in the two interrelated areas of politics and the economy. Certain problems have their roots outside the Continent and therefore are not entirely under the control of those in power or of national leaders. But the Synodal Assembly acknowledged that many of the Continent's problems are the result of a manner of governing often stained by corruption. A serious reawakening of conscience linked to a firm determination of will is necessary, in order to put into effect solutions which can no longer be put off.

Building the nation

111.   On the political front, the arduous process of building national unity encounters particu-

---

[214] Cf. JOHN PAUL II, Encyclical Letter *Sollicitudo Rei Socialis* (30 December 1987), 32: *AAS* 80 (1988), 556.

lar problems in the Continent where most of the States are relatively young political entities. To reconcile profound differences, overcome long-standing ethnic animosities and become integrated into international life demands a high degree of competence in the art of governing. That is why the Synod prayed fervently to the Lord that there would arise in Africa *holy politicians* — both men and women — and that there would be saintly Heads of State, who profoundly love their own people and wish to serve rather than be served.[215]

The rule of law

112.   The foundation of good government must be established on the sound basis of laws which protect the rights and define the obligations of the citizens.[216] I must note with great sadness that many African nations still labour under authoritarian and oppressive regimes which deny their subjects personal freedom and fundamental human rights, especially the freedom of association and of political expression, as well as the right to choose their governments by free and honest elections. Such political injustices provoke tensions which often degenerate into armed conflicts and internal wars, bringing with them serious consequences such as famine, epidemics and destruction, not to mention massacres and the scandal and tragedy of ref-

[215] Cf. *Message of the Synod* (6 May 1994), 35: *L'Osservatore Romano* (English-language edition), 11 May 1994, 8.
[216] Cf. *Propositio* 56.

ugees. That is why the Synod rightly considered that an authentic democracy, which respects pluralism, "is one of the principal routes along which the Church travels together with the people ... The lay Christian, engaged in the democratic struggle according to the spirit of the Gospel, is the sign of a Church which participates in the promotion of the rule of law everywhere in Africa".[217]

Administering the common patrimony

113.   The Synod also called on African governments to establish the appropriate policies needed to increase economic growth and investment in order to create new jobs.[218] This involves the commitment to pursue sound economic policies, adopting the right priorities for the exploitation and distribution of often scarce national resources in such a way as to provide for people's basic needs, and to ensure an honest and equitable sharing of benefits and burdens. In particular, governments have the binding duty to protect the *common patrimony* against all forms of waste and embezzlement by citizens lacking public spirit or by unscrupulous foreigners. It is also the duty of governments to undertake suitable initiatives to improve the conditions of international commerce.

Africa's economic problems are compounded by the dishonesty of corrupt government leaders

---

[217] *Message of the Synod* (6 May 1994), 34: *L'Osservatore Romano* (English-language edition), 11 May 1994, 8.

[218] Cf. *Propositio* 54.

who, in connivance with domestic or foreign private interests, divert national resources for their own profit and transfer public funds to private accounts in foreign banks. This is plain theft, whatever the legal camouflage may be. I earnestly hope that international bodies and people of integrity in Africa and elsewhere will be able to investigate suitable legal ways of having these embezzled funds returned. In the granting of loans, it is important to make sure of the responsibility and forthrightness of the beneficiaries.[219]

The international dimension

114.   As an Assembly of Bishops of the universal Church presided over by the Successor of Peter, the Synod furnished a providential occasion to evaluate positively the place and role of Africa in the universal Church and the world community. Since we live in a world that is increasingly interdependent, the destinies and problems of the different regions are linked together. As God's Family on earth, the Church should be the living sign and efficacious instrument of universal solidarity for building a world-wide community of justice and peace. A better world will come about only if it is built on the solid foundation of sound ethical and spiritual principles.

In the present world order, the African nations are among the most disadvantaged. Rich countries must become clearly aware of their duty

[219] Cf. *ibid.*

to support the efforts of the countries struggling to rise from their poverty and misery. In fact, it is in the interest of the rich countries to choose the path of solidarity, for only in this way can lasting peace and harmony for humanity be ensured. Moreover, the Church in the developed countries cannot ignore the added responsibility arising from the Christian commitment to justice and charity. Because all men and women bear God's image and are called to belong to the same family redeemed by Christ's Blood, each individual should be guaranteed just access to the world's resources which God has put at the everyone's disposal.[220]

It is not hard to see the many practical implications of this. In the first place it involves working for improved socio-political relations among nations, ensuring greater justice and dignity for those countries which, after gaining independence, have been members of the international community for less time. A compassionate ear must also be lent to the anguished cries of the poor nations asking for help in areas of particular importance: malnutrition, the widespread deterioration in the standard of living, the insufficiency of means for educating the young, the lack of elementary health and social services with the resulting persistence of endemic diseases, the

---

[220] Cf. PAUL VI, Encyclical Letter *Populorum Progressio* (26 March 1967): *AAS* 59 (1967), 257-299; JOHN PAUL II, Encyclical Letter *Sollicitudo Rei Socialis* (30 December 1987): *AAS* 80 (1988), 513-586; Encyclical Letter *Centesimus Annus* (1 May 1991): *AAS* 83 (1991), 793-867; *Propositio* 52.

spread of the terrible scourge of AIDS, the heavy and often unbearable burden of international debt, the horror of fratricidal wars fomented by unscrupulous arms trafficking, the shameful and pitiable spectacle of refugees and displaced persons. These are some of the areas where prompt interventions are necessary and expedient, even if in the overall situation they seem to be inadequate.

I. SOME WORRISOME PROBLEMS

Restoring hope to youth

115.   The economic situation of poverty has a particularly negative impact on the young. They embark on adult life with very little enthusiasm for a present riddled with frustrations and they look with still less hope to a future which to them seems sad and sombre. That is why they tend to flee the neglected rural areas and gather in cities which in fact do not have much more to offer them. Many of them go to foreign countries where, as if in exile, they live a precarious existence as economic refugees. With the Synod Fathers I feel the duty to plead their cause: it is urgently necessary to find a solution for their impatience to take part in the life of the nation and of the Church.[221]

But at the same time I also wish to appeal to the youth: Dear young people, the Synod asks you

[221] Cf. SYNOD OF BISHOPS, Special Assembly for Africa, *Message of the Synod* (6 May 1994), 63: *L'Osservatore Romano* (English-language edition), 11 May 1994, 9.

to take in hand the development of your countries, to love the culture of your people, and to work for its renewal with fidelity to your cultural heritage, through a sharpening of your scientific and technical expertise, and above all through the witness of your Christian faith.[222]

The scourge of AIDS

116.   Against the background of widespread poverty and inadequate medical services the Synod considered the tragic scourge of AIDS which is sowing suffering and death in many parts of Africa. It noted the role played in the spread of this disease by irresponsible sexual behaviour and drafted this strong recommendation: "The companionship, joy, happiness and peace which Christian marriage and fidelity provide, and the safeguard which chastity gives, must be continuously presented to the faithful, particularly the young".[223]

The battle against AIDS ought to be everyone's battle. Echoing the voice of the Synod Fathers, I too ask pastoral workers to bring to their brothers and sisters affected by AIDS all possible material, moral and spiritual comfort. I urgently ask the world's scientists and political leaders, moved by the love and respect due to every human person, to use every means available in order to put an end to this scourge.

[222] Cf. ibid.
[223] Propositio 51.

"Beat your swords into ploughshares" (Is 2:4): no more wars!

117. The Synod incisively described the tragedy of wars which are tearing Africa apart: "For
some decades now Africa has been the theatre of
fratricidal wars which are decimating peoples and
destroying their natural and cultural resources".[224]
This very sad situation, in addition to causes external to Africa, also has internal causes such as "tri-
balism, nepotism, racism, religious intolerance and
the thirst for power taken to the extreme by totali-
tarian regimes which trample with impunity the
rights and dignity of the person. Peoples crushed
and reduced to silence suffer as innocent and
resigned victims all these situations of injustice".[225]

I cannot fail to join my voice to that of the
members of the Synodal Assembly in order to de-
plore the situations of unspeakable suffering
caused by so many conflicts now taking place or
about to break out, and to ask all those who can
do so to make every effort to put an end to such
tragedies.

Together with the Synod Fathers, I likewise
urge a serious commitment to foster on the Continent conditions of greater social justice and good
government, in order thereby to prepare the
ground for peace. "If you want peace, work for
justice".[226] It is much better — and also easier

---

[224] *Propositio* 45.
[225] *Ibid.*
[226] PAUL VI, Address at Boys' Town for the Fifth World Day of
Peace (1 January 1972): *AAS* 64 (1972), 44.

— to prevent wars than to try to stop them after they have broken out. It is time that peoples beat their swords into ploughshares, and their spears into pruning hooks (cf. *Is* 2:4).

118.   The Church in Africa — especially through some of its leaders — has been in the front line of the search for negotiated solutions to the armed conflicts in many parts of the Continent. This mission of pacification must continue, encouraged by the Lord's promise in the Beatitudes: "Blessed are the peacemakers, they shall be called sons of God" (*Mt* 5:9).

Those who foment wars in Africa by the arms trade are accomplices in abominable crimes against humanity. I make my own the Synod's recommendations on this subject. Having said that "the sale of arms is a scandal since it sows the seed of death", the Synod appealed to all countries that sell arms to Africa to stop doing so, and it asked African governments "to move away from huge military expenditures and put the emphasis on the education, health and well-being of their people".[227]

Africa must continue to seek peaceful and effective means so that military regimes will transfer authority to civilians. But it is also true that the military are called to play a distinctive role in the nation. Thus, while the Synod praised the "brothers in the military for the service that they assume in the name of our countries",[228] it im-

---

[227] *Propositio* 49.
[228] *Message of the Synod* (6 May 1994), 35: *L'Osservatore Romano* (English-language edition), 11 May 1994, 8.

mediately warned them forcefully that "they will have to answer before God for every act of violence against the lives of innocent people".[229]

Refugees and displaced persons

119.   One of the most bitter fruits of wars and economic hardships is the sad phenomenon of refugees and displaced persons, a phenomenon which, as the Synod mentioned, has reached tragic dimensions. The ideal solution is the re-establishment of a just peace, reconciliation and economic development. It is therefore urgent that national, regional and international organizations should find equitable and long-lasting solutions to the problems of refugees and displaced persons.[230] In the meantime, since the Continent continues to suffer from the massive displacement of refugees, I make a pressing appeal that these people be given material help and offered pastoral support wherever they may be, whether in Africa or on other Continents.

The burden of the international debt

120.   The question of the indebtedness of poor nations towards rich ones is a matter of great concern for the Church, as expressed in many official documents and interventions of the Holy See.[231]

---

[229] Ibid.

[230] Cf. Propositio 53.

[231] Cf. SECOND VATICAN ECUMENICAL COUNCIL, Pastoral Constitution on the Church in the Modern World Gaudium et Spes, 86;

Taking up the words of the Synod Fathers, I particularly feel it is my duty to urge "the Heads of State and their governments in Africa not to crush their peoples with internal and external debts".[232] I also make a pressing appeal to "the International Monetary Fund and the World Bank and all foreign creditors to alleviate the crushing debts of the African nations".[233] Finally, I earnestly ask "the Episcopal Conferences of the industrialized countries to present this issue consistently to their governments and to the organizations concerned".[234] The situation of many African countries is so serious as to leave no room for attitudes of indifference and complacency.

Dignity of the African woman

121.   One of the characteristic signs of our times is the growing awareness of women's dignity and of their specific role in the Church and in society at large. "So God created man in his own

PAUL VI, Encyclical Letter *Populorum Progressio* (26 March 1967), 54: *AAS* 59 (1967), 283-284; JOHN PAUL II, Encyclical Letter *Sollicitudo Rei Socialis* (30 December 1987), 19: *AAS* 80 (1988), 534-536; Encyclical Letter *Centesimus Annus* (1 May 1991), 35: *AAS* 83 (1991), 836-838; Apostolic Letter *Tertio Millennio Adveniente* (10 November 1994), 51: *AAS* 87 (1995), 36, which proposes as part of the preparation for the Great Jubilee of the Year 2000 "reducing substantially, if not cancelling outright, the international debt which seriously threatens the future of many nations"; PONTIFICAL COMMISSION "IUSTITIA ET PAX", *At the Service of the Human Community: An Ethical Approach to the International Debt Question* (27 December 1986): Vatican City, 1986.

[232] *Propositio* 49.
[233] *Ibid.*
[234] *Ibid.*

image, in the image of God he created him; male and female he created them" (*Gen* 1:27).

I have repeatedly affirmed the fundamental equality and enriching complementarity that exist between man and woman.[235] The Synod applied these principles to the condition of women in Africa. Their rights and duties in building up the family and in taking full part in the development of the Church and society were strongly affirmed. With specific regard to the Church, women should be properly trained so that they can participate at appropriate levels in her apostolic activity.

The Church deplores and condemns, to the extent that they are still found in some African societies, all "the customs and practices which deprive women of their rights and the respect due to them".[236] It is recommended that Episcopal Conferences establish special commissions to study further women's problems in cooperation with interested government agencies, wherever this is possible.[237]

II. COMMUNICATING THE GOOD NEWS

Following Christ, the Communicator "par excellence"

122.   The Synod had much to say about social communications in the context of the evangeliza-

---

[235] Cf. Apostolic Letter *Mulieris Dignitatem* (15 August 1988), 6-8: *AAS* 80 (1988), 1662-1670; *Letter to Women* (29 June 1995), 7: *L'Osservatore Romano* (English-language edition), 12 July 1995, 2.

[236] *Propositio* 48.

[237] Cf. *ibid.*

tion of Africa, carefully taking into account present circumstances. The theological point of departure is Christ, the Communicator *par excellence* who shares with those who believe in him the truth, the life and the love which he shares with his Heavenly Father and the Holy Spirit. That is why "the Church is aware of her duty of fostering social communications *ad intra* and *ad extra*. The Church should promote communication from within through a better diffusion of information among her members".[238] This will put her in a more advantageous position to communicate to the world the Good News of the love of God revealed in Jesus Christ.

Traditional forms of communication

123. The traditional forms of social communication must never be underestimated. In many places in Africa they are still very useful and effective. Moreover, they are "less costly and more accessible".[239] These forms include songs and music, mimes and the theatre, proverbs and fables. As vehicles of the wisdom and soul of the people, they are a precious source of material and of inspiration for the modern media.

Evangelization of the world of the media

124. The modern mass media are not only instruments of communication, but also a world to

---

[238] *Propositio* 57.
[239] *Ibid*.

be evangelized. In terms of the message they transmit, it is necessary to ensure that they propagate the good, the true and the beautiful. Echoing the preoccupation of the Synod Fathers I express my deep concern about the moral content of very many programmes with which the media flood the African Continent. In particular I warn against the pornography and violence which are inundating poor countries. In addition, the Synod rightly deplored "the very negative portrayal of the African in the media and called for its immediate cessation".[240]

Every Christian should be concerned that the communications media are a vehicle of evangelization. But Christians who are professionals in this sector have a special part to play. It is their duty to ensure that Christian principles influence the practice of the profession, including the technical and administrative sector. To enable them to exercise this role properly, they need to be provided with a wholesome human, religious and spiritual training.

Using the means of social communication

125. Today the Church has at her disposal a variety of means of social communication, traditional as well as modern. It is her duty to make the best possible use of them in order to spread the message of salvation. In the Church in Africa many obstacles impede easy access to these means,

[240] *Propositio* 61.

not the least of which is their high cost. Moreover, in many places government regulations impose undue control on them. Every possible effort should be made to remove these obstacles. The media, whether private or public, should serve all people without exception. Therefore I invite the particular Churches of Africa to do everything in their power to meet this objective.[241]

Cooperation and coordination in the mass media

126. The media, especially in their most modern forms, have a wide-ranging impact. Consequently, closer cooperation is needed in this area, in order to ensure more effective coordination at all levels: diocesan, national, continental and worldwide. In Africa, the Church has a great need for solidarity with sister Churches in the richer and technologically more advanced countries. Programmes of continental cooperation which already exist in Africa, such as the Pan African Episcopal Committee for Social Communications, should be encouraged and revitalized. As the Synod suggested, it is necessary to establish closer cooperation in other areas, such as professional training, structures of radio and television production, and stations that transmit to the whole Continent.[242]

---

[241] Cf. *Propositio* 58.
[242] Cf. *Propositio* 60.

"YOU SHALL BE MY WITNESSES
TO THE ENDS OF THE EARTH"

127. During the Special Assembly, the Synod Fathers thoroughly explored the overall situation in Africa, in order to encourage an ever more effective and credible witness to Christ in every local Church, every nation, every region, and in the entire African Continent. In all the discussions and recommendations made by the Special Assembly the overriding concern was to *bear witness to Christ*. I found in them the spirit of what I had said in Africa to a group of Bishops: "By respecting, preserving and fostering the particular values and riches of your people's cultural heritage, you will be in a position to lead them to a better understanding of the mystery of Christ, which is also to be lived in the noble, concrete and daily experiences of African life. There is no question of adulterating the word of God, or of emptying the Cross of its power (cf. *1 Cor* 1:17), but rather of bringing Christ into the very centre of African life and of lifting up all African life to Christ. Thus not only is Christianity relevant to Africa, but

Christ, in the members of his Body, is himself African".[243]

Open to mission

128.   The Church in Africa is not called to bear witness to Christ only on the Continent; for to it the Risen Lord also says: "You shall be my witnesses to the ends of the earth" (*Acts* 1:8). For this very reason, during their discussions of the Synod's theme, the Fathers carefully avoided every tendency to isolationism by the Church in Africa. At all times the Special Assembly kept in view the missionary mandate which the Church received from Christ: to bear witness to him in the whole world.[244] The Synod Fathers acknowledged God's call to Africa to play its full part, at the world level, in his plan for the salvation of the human race (cf. *1 Tim* 2:4).

129.   It is on account of this commitment to the Church's catholicity that the *Lineamenta* of the Special Assembly for Africa declared: "No particular Church, not even the poorest, can ever be dispensed from the obligation of sharing its personnel as well as its spiritual and temporal resources with other particular Churches and with the universal Church (cf. *Acts* 2:44-45)".[245] For its part, the Special Assembly strongly stressed Afri-

---

[243] Address to the Bishops of Kenya, Nairobi (7 May 1980), 6: *AAS* 72 (1980), 497.
[244] Cf. PAUL VI, Apostolic Exhortation *Evangelii Nuntiandi* (8 December 1975), 50: *AAS* 68 (1976), 40.
[245] No. 42.

ca's responsibility for mission "to the ends of the earth" in the following words: "The prophetic phrase of Paul VI, 'You Africans are missionaries to yourselves', is to be understood as 'missionaries to the whole world' ... An appeal is launched to the particular Churches of Africa for mission outside the confines of their own Dioceses".[246]

130.   In gladly and gratefully endorsing this declaration of the Special Assembly, I wish to repeat to all my Brother Bishops in Africa what I said a few years ago: "The Church in Africa's obligation to be missionary to itself and to evangelize the Continent entails cooperation among the particular Churches in the context of each African country, among the various nations of the Continent and also of other continents. In this way Africa will be fully integrated in missionary activity".[247] In an earlier appeal addressed to all the particular Churches, both young and old, I already said that "the world is steadily growing more united, and the Gospel spirit must lead us to overcome cultural and nationalistic barriers, avoiding all isolationism".[248]

The bold determination manifested by the Special Assembly to engage the young Churches of Africa in mission "to the ends of the earth" reflects the desire to implement, as generously as

---

[246] *Relatio post disceptationem* (22 April 1994), 11: *L'Osservatore Romano*, 24 April 1994, 8.

[247] Address to the Episcopal Conference of Senegal, Mauritania, Cape Verde and Guinea-Bissau, Poponguine (20 February 1992), 3: *AAS* 85 (1993), 150.

[248] Encyclical Letter *Redemptoris Missio* (7 December 1990), 39: *AAS* 83 (1991), 287.

possible, one of the important directives of the Second Vatican Council: "In order that this missionary zeal may flourish among their native members, it very fitting that the young Churches should participate as soon as possible in the universal missionary work of the Church. Let them send their own missionaries to proclaim the Gospel all over the world, even though they themselves are suffering from a shortage of clergy. For their communion with the universal Church reaches a certain measure of perfection when they themselves take an active part in missionary zeal towards other nations".[249]

Organic pastoral solidarity

131.   At the beginning of this Exhortation I pointed out that in announcing the convocation of the Special Assembly for Africa of the Synod of Bishops I had in mind the promotion of "an organic pastoral solidarity within the entire African territory and nearby Islands".[250] I am pleased to say that the Assembly kept this objective firmly in view. Discussions at the Synod revealed the Bishops' readiness and generosity for this pastoral solidarity and for sharing their resources with others, even when they themselves needed missionaries.

132.   Specifically to my brother Bishops, who "are directly responsible, together with me, for the

---

[249] Decree on the Missionary Activity of the Church *Ad Gentes*, 20.
[250] Angelus (6 January 1989), 2: *Insegnamenti* XII/1 (1989), 40.

evangelization of the world, both as members of the College of Bishops and as Pastors of the particular Churches",[251] I wish to address a special word in this regard. In their daily ministry to the flock entrusted to them, they must never lose sight of the needs of the Church as a whole. As *Catholic* Bishops, they must feel the concern for all the Churches which burned in the Apostle's heart (cf. *2 Cor* 11:28). Nor can they fail to express this concern, especially when they deliberate and decide *together* as members of their respective Episcopal Conferences. Through liaison bodies at the regional and continental levels, they are in a better position to discern and evaluate the pastoral needs surfacing in other parts of the world. The Bishops express their apostolic solidarity in a pre-eminent way through the Synod of Bishops: "among its affairs of general concern, it should give special consideration to missionary activity. For this is a supremely great and sacred task of the Church".[252]

133.   The Special Assembly also rightly pointed out that, in order to achieve an overall pastoral solidarity in Africa, it is necessary to promote the renewal of priestly formation. The words of the Second Vatican Council can never be pondered enough: "The spiritual gift which priests received at their Ordination prepares them not for any limited and narrow mission but for the widest scope

---

[251] JOHN PAUL II, Encyclical Letter *Redemptoris Missio* (7 December 1990), 63: *AAS* 83 (1991), 311.
[252] SECOND VATICAN ECUMENICAL COUNCIL, Decree on the Missionary Activity of the Church *Ad Gentes*, 29.

of the universal mission 'even to the very ends of the earth' (*Acts* 1:8)".[253]

That is why I have urged priests "to make themselves readily available to the Holy Spirit and the Bishop, to be sent to preach the Gospel beyond the borders of their own country. This will demand of them not only maturity in their vocation, but also an uncommon readiness to detach themselves from their own homeland, culture and family, and a special ability to adapt to other cultures, with understanding and respect for them".[254]

I am deeply grateful to God to learn that a growing number of African priests have been responding to the call to bear witness "to the ends of the earth". It is my ardent hope that this trend will be encouraged and strengthened in all the particular Churches of Africa.

134.   It is also a source of great comfort to know that the Missionary Institutes which have been present in Africa for a long time are now "receiving more and more candidates from the young Churches which they founded",[255] thus enabling these same Churches to take part in the missionary activity of the universal Church. Similarly, I give thanks for the new Missionary Institutes which have been established on the Continent and are now sending their members

[253] Decree on the Ministry and Life of Priests *Presbyterorum Ordinis*, 10.

[254] Encyclical Letter *Redemptoris Missio* (7 December 1990), 67: *AAS* 83 (1991), 316.

[255] *Ibid.*, 66: *loc. cit.*, 314.

ad gentes. This is a providential and marvellous development which shows the maturity and dynamism of the Church in Africa.

135. In a special way I would like to endorse the specific recommendation of the Synod Fathers that the four Pontifical Mission Aid Societies be established in every particular Church and in every country as a means of achieving an *organic pastoral solidarity* in favour of the mission "to the ends of the earth". These Societies, because they are under the auspices of the Pope and the Episcopal College, rightly have the first place, "since they are the means of imbuing Catholics from their very infancy with a genuinely universal and missionary outlook. They are the means for undertaking an effective collection of funds to subsidize all the missions, each according to its needs".[256] A significant result of their activity "is the fostering of lifelong vocations *ad gentes,* in both the older and younger Churches. I earnestly recommend that their promotional work be increasingly directed to this goal".[257]

Holiness and mission

136. The Synod reaffirmed that all the sons and daughters of Africa are called to holiness and to be witnesses to Christ throughout the world.

[256] SECOND VATICAN ECUMENICAL COUNCIL, Decree on the Missionary Activity of the Church *Ad Gentes,* 38.

[257] Encyclical Letter *Redemptoris Missio* (7 December 1990), 84: *AAS* 83 (1991), 331.

"The lesson of history confirms that by the action of the Holy Spirit evangelization takes place above all through the witness of charity, the *witness of holiness*".[258] I therefore wish to repeat to all Christians in Africa what I wrote some years ago: "A missionary is really such only if he commits himself to the way of holiness ... Every member of the faithful is called to holiness and to mission ... The renewed impulse to the mission *ad gentes* demands holy missionaries. It is not enough to update pastoral techniques, organize and coordinate ecclesial resources, or delve deeply into the biblical and theological foundations of faith. What is needed is the encouragement of a new 'ardour for holiness' among missionaries and throughout the Christian community".[259]

As I did then, so again I address myself to the Christians of the young Churches in order to remind them of their responsibilities: "Today, you are the hope of this two-thousand-year-old Church of ours: being young in faith, you must be like the first Christians and radiate enthusiasm and courage. In a word, you must set yourselves on the path of holiness. Only thus can you be a sign of God in the world and re-live in your own countries the missionary epic of the early Church. You will also be a leaven of missionary spirit for the older Churches".[260]

[258] JOHN PAUL II, Address to a group of Bishops of Nigeria during their *ad Limina* Visit (21 January 1982), 4: *AAS* 74 (1982), 435-436.

[259] Encyclical Letter *Redemptoris Missio* (7 December 1990), 90: *AAS* 83 (1991), 336-337.

[260] *Ibid.*, 91: *loc. cit.*, 337-338.

137.   The Church in Africa shares with the universal Church "the sublime vocation of realizing, first of all within herself, the unity of humankind over and above any ethnic, cultural, national, social or other divisions in order to signify precisely that such divisions are now obsolete, having been abolished by the Cross of Christ".[261] By responding to her vocation to be a redeemed and reconciled people in the midst of the world, the Church contributes to promoting the fraternal coexistence of all peoples, since she transcends the distinctions of race and nationality.

In view of the specific vocation entrusted to the Church by her Divine Founder, I earnestly call upon the Catholic Community in Africa to bear authentic witness before all humanity to the Christian universalism which has its source in the fatherhood of God. "All persons created by God have the same *origin*. Whatever may, throughout history, have been their dispersion or the accentuation of their differences, they are *destined* to form one sole family according to God's plan established 'in the beginning' ".[262] The Church in Africa is called to reach out in love to every human being, firmly believing that "by his Incarnation the Son of God has united himself in some fashion with every man".[263]

[261] PONTIFICAL COMMISSION "IUSTITIA ET PAX", *The Church and Racism: Towards a More Fraternal Society* (3 November 1988), 22: Vatican City, 1988.

[262] *Ibid.*, 20: *loc. cit.*

[263] SECOND VATICAN ECUMENICAL COUNCIL, Pastoral Constitution on the Church in the Modern World *Gaudium et Spes, 22.*

In particular, Africa ought to make its own special contribution to the ecumenical movement, an urgent task which, on the threshold of the Third Millennium, I have emphasized once more in my Encyclical Letter *Ut Unum Sint*.[264] Certainly the Church on the Continent can also play an important role in interreligious dialogue, above all by fostering close relations with Muslims and by promoting respect for the values of African traditional religion.

Putting solidarity into practice

138. In bearing witness to Christ "to the ends of the earth", the Church in Africa will no doubt be assisted by the conviction of the "*positive* and *moral value* of the growing awareness of *interdependence* among individuals and nations. The fact that men and women in various parts of the world feel personally affected by the injustices and violations of human rights committed in distant countries, countries which perhaps they will never visit, is a further sign of a reality transformed into *awareness*, thus acquiring a *moral* connotation".[265]

It is my desire that Christians in Africa will become ever more aware of this interdependence among individuals and nations, and will be ready to respond to it by practising the virtue of *solidarity*. The fruit of solidarity is peace, an inestimable

---

[264] Nos. 77-79: *L'Osservatore Romano* (English-language edition), 31 May 1995, Special Supplement, XI.
[265] JOHN PAUL II, Encyclical Letter *Sollicitudo Rei Socialis* (30 December 1987), 38: *AAS* 80 (1988), 565.

good for peoples and nations in every part of the world. For it is precisely by means of fostering and strengthening solidarity that the Church can make a specific and decisive contribution to a true culture of peace.

139. By entering into contact with all the peoples of the world through her dialogue with the various cultures, the Church brings them closer to one another, enabling each people to assume, in faith, the authentic values of others.

Ready to cooperate with all people of good will and with the international community, the Church in Africa does not seek advantages for itself. The solidarity which it expresses "seeks to go beyond itself, to take on the *specifically Christian* dimensions of total gratuity, forgiveness and reconciliation".[266] The Church seeks to contribute to humanity's conversion, leading it to acceptance of God's salvific plan through her witness to the Gospel, accompanied by charitable work on behalf of the poor and the neediest. In so doing she never loses sight of the primacy of the transcendent and of those spiritual realities which are the first fruits of man's eternal salvation.

In their discussion on the Church's solidarity with peoples and nations, the Synod Fathers were at all times fully aware that "earthly progress must be carefully distinguished from the growth of Christ's Kingdom. Nevertheless, to the extent that the former can contribute to the better ordering

---

[266] *Ibid.*, 40: *loc. cit.*, 568.

present Exhortation I invite God's People in Africa — Bishops, priests, consecrated persons and lay faithful — to set their faces resolutely towards the Great Jubilee which we shall celebrate a few years hence. For all the peoples of Africa the best preparation for the new Millennium must consist in a firm commitment to implement with great fidelity the decisions and orientations which, with the Apostolic authority of the Successor of Peter, I present in this Exhortation. They are decisions and orientations which can be traced back to the genuine heritage of the Church's teaching and discipline and in particular to the Second Vatican Council, the main source of inspiration for the Special Assembly for Africa.

142. My invitation to God's People in Africa to prepare themselves for the Great Jubilee of the Year 2000 is also meant to be *a clarion call to Christian joy.* "The great joy announced by the angel on Christmas night is truly for all the people (cf. *Lk* 2:10) ... The Blessed Virgin Mary was the first to have received its announcement, from the Angel Gabriel, and her *Magnificat* was already the exultant hymn of all the humble. Whenever we say the Rosary, the joyful mysteries thus place us once more before the inexpressible event which is the centre and summit of history: the coming on earth of Emmanuel, God with us".[269]

It is the two thousandth Anniversary of that event of great joy which we are preparing to cele-

[269] PAUL VI, Apostolic Exhortation *Gaudete in Domino* (9 May 1975), III: *AAS* 67 (1975), 297.

brate with the coming Great Jubilee. And so Africa, which "is also in a sense the 'second homeland' of Jesus, since as a small child, it was there that he sought refuge from Herod's cruelty",[270] is called to joy. At the same time, "everything ought to focus on the primary objective of the Jubilee: *the strengthening of faith and of the witness of Christians*".[271]

143. On account of the many difficulties, crises and conflicts which bring about so much suffering and misery on the Continent, some Africans are at times tempted to think that the Lord has abandoned them, that he has forgotten them (cf. *Is* 49:14)! "And God answers with the words of the great Prophet: 'Can a woman forget her own baby and not love the child she bore? Even if a mother should forget a child, I will never forget you. I have written your names on the palms of my hands' (*Is* 49:15-16). Yes, on the palms of Christ, pierced by the nails of the Crucifixion. The names of each one of you [Africans] is written on those palms. Therefore with full confidence we cry out: 'The Lord is our help and our shield. In him do our hearts find joy. We trust in his holy name' (*Ps* 28:7)".[272]

---

[270] JOHN PAUL II, Homily at the Opening Mass of the Special Assembly for Africa of the Synod of Bishops (10 April 1994), 1: *AAS* 87 (1995), 179.

[271] JOHN PAUL II, Apostolic Letter *Tertio Millennio Adveniente* (10 November 1994), 42: *AAS* 87 (1995), 32.

[272] JOHN PAUL II, Homily at Mass, Khartoum (10 February 1993), 8: *AAS* 85 (1993), 964.

Prayer to Mary, Mother of the Church

144.   In thanksgiving for the grace of this
Synod, I appeal to Mary, Star of Evangelization
and, as the Third Millennium draws near, to her I
entrust Africa and its evangelizing mission. I turn
to her with the thoughts and sentiments expressed
in the prayer which my Brother Bishops com-
posed at the close of the working session of the
Synod in Rome:

O Mary, Mother of God
and Mother of the Church,
thanks to you, on the day of the Annunciation,
at the dawn of the new era,
the whole human race with its cultures
rejoiced in recognizing itself
ready for the Gospel.
On the eve of a new Pentecost
for the Church in Africa, Madagascar
and the adjacent Islands,
the People of God with its Pastors
turns to you and with you fervently prays:
May the outpouring of the Holy Spirit
make of the cultures of Africa
places of communion in diversity,
fashioning the peoples
of this great Continent
into generous sons and daughters
of the Church
which is the Family of the Father,
the Brotherhood of the Son,
the Image of the Trinity,

the seed and beginning on earth
of the eternal Kingdom
which will come to its perfection
in the City that has God as its Builder:
the City of justice, love and peace.

Given at Yaoundé, in Cameroon, on 14 September, Feast of the Triumph of the Cross, in the year 1995, the seventeenth of my Pontificate.

Joannes Paulus II